ROAD TO ITHAKA

A MEMOIR

DIANE CAMPBELL THOMPSON

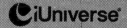

ROAD TO ITHAKA
A MEMOIR

iUniverse books may be ordered through booksellers or by contacting:

iUniverse
1663 Liberty Drive
Bloomington, IN 47403
www.iuniverse.com
1-800-Authors (1-800-288-4677)

ISBN: 978-1-4917-5503-7 (sc)
ISBN: 978-1-4917-5504-4 (e)

Printed in the United States of America.

iUniverse rev. date: 01/30/2015

CONTENTS

AUTHOR'S NOTE

The purpose of this book is to record events as they actually happened. All of the stories are true and are from my own memories.

Material which is copied directly from my personal journals appears in italics.

I have changed some of the names to protect myself from lawsuits and others from embarrassment.

PREFACE

"Unabridged Journals" such as those of Sylvia Plath, Lucy Maud Montgomery, Anne Frank and others even less well known make intensely interesting reading. Historians in their research benefit from such journals. Personal memoirs can tell us something of the life and times of the writer.

The first diary I ever kept was at the age of eleven. A small pocket edition with just a half inch of space per day I wrote in thick adolescent scrawl one line entries "went to school" "tea at Brenda's" "not talking to Wendy." From that I graduated to covered diaries that came with a key. Safe to write secrets here and erratic words flowed profusely. Today my journals are large letter size notebooks recounting the daily comings and goings of an ordinary life. Each year my efforts have become more expansive, drawings, calligraphic flourishes, newspaper clippings, experiments with paint emerge and then, in a quest to simply write better I signed on to a Journal Writing course.

I came to the course wide eyed and with the curiosity of Alice. I had no idea what to expect or what was expected of me, I knew only that I was long past a school-room and homework. Required reading of *"The Blue Jay's Dance" by Louise Erdrich* caused the first flutter of panic. The assignment was a book review, something I had absolutely no experience of. Reading the book feverishly, trying to digest it thoroughly, I made copious notes. To identify structure, context and metaphors started to give me a headache. Not confident of my first summation I read the book again and magic began! A tiny light flickered in my head. Yes! Here is the structure and there the symbols and the metaphors. It was marvellous, but how is it I had never noticed them before? I went straight down-stairs and picked up an armful of books from my shelves, not entirely convinced all authors used these methods. I began reading like mad. My bedside became a dizzying shamble of leaning book towers. Coil bound notebooks were scribbled in furiously. I began to identify examples in all of the books the principles of writing outlined in the course lecture. Suddenly I seemed to be reading in a new way. Nights became restless; never a serial dreamer, I was visited by unknown faces, nagging voices and my mind kept stabbing into vacant air to find metaphors of my own. The more I tried the more I became convinced mine was a hopeless case, all the great metaphors and symbols were used up, there was simply none left for me to invent.

Each Friday with a new assignment posted I welcomed the task of a new challenge. Subjects pushed me down avenues I had not previously thought to explore. People and events in my life shifted in perspective. Some assignments dug up buried emotions and I found myself typing into a laptop with stinging eyes. My stories, dreams and myths had a central theme; earth's natural beauty, a Lorelei song tramping through a forest of trees, paddling a glassy lake or standing on an untamed shore. My dream and wishes assignment told me that life so far has brought me to a place of humble contentment. There is time now for introspection. Writing character caused me to consider more deeply those people around me, to try to see behind the masks of convention and society. I am still on a search for self and am a complicated sum of those same people and the world around me.

After submitting an assignment, the instructor's review would follow and appear in the personal mail-box. Sitting alone at my lap-top, I take a deep breath and dare myself to dial up the college connection. That little red flag always gives a shudder. Squirming in my seat, I feel something akin to sitting in a dentist chair dreading that long needle which will freeze my mouth "Just a little prick." I download the email from Kathryn. The pain is brief; my jaw drops in surprise, the remarks are, well, encouraging.

Now that the course is ended I fear I shall fall back to the old lack lustre entries. I will miss the provocative assignments. I have come quite a long way from the everyday rants that were taking over my journals. Building structure, creating scenes, showing not telling, writing between the lines and those darn metaphors are front and center as I try to become a better writer. My mind is a mansion with many rooms. People and events are locked inside these rooms and are banging on the doors to be set free. Through this course I managed to open a few doors and let some of them out, so that the noise has subsided somewhat. But there are still many rooms to be aired and the occupants have settled down, knowing that in the fullness of time, each will have a chance to get out.

The inspiration to write this book came from that journal course. I have tried to give a fair and honest account of my life so far. The journals reflect my life and thoughts at that time and my hope is that future generations will have some insight into the world in which I was raised. I still have much to learn on the art of writing and I have many more stories to tell of course, but they must wait for another day.

CHILDHOOD

KEEP CALM AND CARRY ON.

A toddler with a curly bob of black hair is watching a mother pulling together heavy dark curtains. They hang with small brass rings from a bamboo rod and the mother is sliding them closed with another tall bamboo rod, they are long black curtains. Outside, under a darkening sky, a father is busy banging faded green wooden shutters over downstairs windows. Each shutter bangs loudly as he moves around the house; when he comes to the open back door he will call my name, "Diane!" Although it is night-time, I am not going up to my bed; a siren is wailing and I run to him, we are going out. I am used to this routine and sense the soberness that cloaks us.

On the 1st of September 1939 Germany invaded Poland and two days later Britain and France declared war on Germany; this was the beginning of World War 11 which wouldn't end until 2nd September 1945. I was born 30th May 1941.

Few raids were made on England in 1939, but in the late summer of 1940 German bombers for the first time started raids on dockyards. My father was an engineer on the Grimsby docks. Hitler planned to invade Britain and in September 1940 the Germans started bombing cities instead of RAF air bases. Between September 1940 and May 1941, the Luftwaffe made 127 large scale night raids. Of these 71 were targeted on London. The main targets outside of London were Liverpool, Birmingham, Plymouth, Bristol, Glasgow, Southampton, Coventry, Portsmouth, Manchester, Belfast, Sheffield, Newcastle, Nottingham, Cardiff and Hull. Of these, Hull was just across the river from Grimsby and both towns were major fishing ports. I was born in Grimsby. While Hitler did bomb Grimsby extensively, he did not want the town totally destroyed as his invasion plan included a landing there. They especially wanted to avoid Dock Tower as they used it as a navigation aid, so much so that the British government considered bombing it themselves. You can find a German surveillance map of the town at *http://www.rodcollins.com/wordpress/wartime-bombing-in-grimsby-lincolnshire-with-unique-maps.*

I was born at number five Tyler Avenue in the town centre and in the middle of one of the Luftwaffe air-raids. Of course, I don't remember this, but my parents have told me many times that my arrival coincided with a special email from Adolph Hitler, so you see; I can truly boast that I arrived with a bang! (And some would say, have been causing a disturbance ever since). My father, who was in the Home Guard (popularized in the BBC comedy series *Dad's Army*), stood on guard outside the house waiting to rush mom and me into the air-raid shelter. My bed that night was a wooden bench in a tiny air-raid shelter and before the war ended I would spend many a night thus. Shortly after my birth, we moved to the countryside just outside of town and closer to the North Sea Shore.

Raids were a nightly business in what has come to be known as the "Great Blitz" (from the German word, "lightning"). As soon as the incoming bombers were spotted in the sky, air raid sirens warned everyone that a raid was on the way. The alert itself was an up and down howling sound and went on for about three minutes. The all clear was a single note. When the raid was over people would emerge from their shelters to find that some of their homes had been completely flattened. Others found dead or injured relatives. We were one of the lucky ones who escaped such horror. The Germans showered Britain with bombs, fire bombs, delayed action bombs and anti-personnel butterfly bombs. The police, the fire fighters, bomb disposal men, ambulance drivers and ARP (Air Raid Protection wardens) were all kept very busy. Some people hid under tables in their home, or in cellars, or under the stairs as my grandmother did and some like us had a shelter in the garden. On 14 June 1943, an early morning air raid by the Luftwaffe saw several 1,000 kg bombs, 6,000 incendiary bombs and more than 3,000 Butterfly Bombs fall in the Grimsby area. That night 99 of the 196 killed by WW11 bombing raids in Grimsby and Cleethorpes lost their lives and 184 people were seriously injured. In 1944, Britain faced attacks from new weapons. First the *V-1*, a robot 'flying bomb,' then there was the *V-2*; a rocket which flew so fast no-one could see or hear it coming. London was the main target for V-1 and V-2 attacks.

Like so many, we had an air-raid shelter to hide in when the raids started. Our shelter sat close to the house and was nestled next to a tall scraggly hawthorn hedge. On the other side of the hedge lived our neighbours Mr. and Mrs. Finch, who shared the shelter with us. They were an elderly couple. Mr. Finch was a frail looking seventy year old who walked with a stoop and whose angular face, large hawkish eyes and pointed nose gave him the look of an eagle. He was a cheerful character, while his new wife Alice was a tad younger with small twinkling blue eyes, black shoulder length hair swept back into a fashionable roll and a plump face. Alice loved to sew and made me many small presents; a golliwog made from old socks and an exquisite silk and lace heart in which to store handkerchiefs. The picture of those two old people is very dear to my mind and I can see them now as they sat together in the shelter each night.

My memory of those toddler years is crystal clear; standing at the open kitchen door I am looking up at my father who is dressed in camouflage and wearing a tin hat. He scoops me up with his right arm and in his left hand is a brown paper bag (sandwiches for the night). He hoists me over his shoulder and as we go to the shelter just a few feet away I can see search lights criss-crossing the sky. I hear planes and the drone of the Lancaster bomber, that familiar drone now marked indelibly in my soul. Over the docks on the near horizon floats a large barrage balloon. I am carried into the shelter and deposited on the wooden bench on the left hand side. Mr. and Mrs. Finch are already there, sitting close together on the back bench. There is the tiniest oil lamp; it's like a doll's lamp, barely six inches tall, with a green tin bottom and a milky glass bowl shade. Many years later while digging in the garden we will unearth this little lamp which now flickers low in the dark and is our only source of light. My mother follows us into the shelter and closes the wooden door which she then covers completely with a large sack. The sack will prevent any light from the tiny lamp leaking outside. Blackouts are strictly enforced every night. Inside the shelter it is very small and the roof curves over making it feel like being in a tunnel. There is nothing for us to do in the darkness but sit and look at each other. My father is no longer here and outside the frightening sound of war, bombs, guns and planes. It causes fear and staring wide - eyed at the sack I feel sure 'they' will break down the door at any minute; I think they may be walking round our garden shed and I have no idea who 'they' are.

Maybe I fell asleep in the shelter and maybe when the all-clear siren sounded I was carried back into the house to sleep until daylight came. I don't remember coming out only going in. Come out we did though and go back in again the next night and I would struggle with nightmares for many years after.

The shelters were tin huts called *Anderson Shelters*. One and a half million of these shelters were distributed to people expected to be bombed by the Luftwaffe. They were made from curved steel sheets bolted together at the top. They measured 6'6" (1.98m) by 4' 6" (1.37m). Issued free to the poor, men who earned more than five pound a week could buy one for seven pounds. By the time of the Blitz, two and quarter million families had an Anderson shelter in the garden. When the Luftwaffe changed to night bombing raids from daylight, people were expected to sleep in the shelters. Each night the wail of the sirens announced an oncoming invasion, giving people time to take cover before the raid started. The shelters were cold and damp and prone to flooding as ours did. Neither was the shelter even slightly soundproof. Another form of indoor shelter was the Morrison shelter, officially termed *Table (Morrison) Indoor Shelter* and had a cage-like construction. The shelters came in kits to be bolted together inside the home. They were approximately 6 ft. 6 in (2 m) long, 4 ft. (1.2 m) wide and 2 ft. 6 in (0.75 m) high, had a solid 1/8 in (3 mm) steel plate 'table' top, welded wire mesh sides and a metal lath 'mattress' - type floor. Two people could lie comfortably side by side in this cage, but that is all, it was not even high enough for someone to sit up in and looked like a large dog cage.

The town of Grimsby was heavily sandbagged; road signs were removed to confuse the Germans and nightly blackouts were in effect. Anything that could be done to impede and confuse the invading German army was put into motion. Large concrete bollards called "Dragons Teeth" were placed along some roads, which were meant to make roads impassable for the impending enemy tanks and vehicles.

In town, the damage was severe. On weekly visits to visit my grandmother Anderson who lived close to the docks we were reduced to stepping over and around the rubble of fallen homes. Whole streets were obliterated and the acrid smell of ash was everywhere. Children, dirty and ragged played among the ruins. The streets stayed in this condition for many years after the war, for I remember visiting there with my brother and sister and stepping around the bomb buildings. We were always forbidden to play outside in these ruins, much to my chagrin. I was fascinated by the inside of these forlorn skeletons and curiously stared up to see what kind of wallpaper they had used, or sometimes to a picture still hanging on what was left of a bedroom wall. On my grandmother's street, which was called Levington Street, many of the houses were in ruins. By some twist of fate, my grandmother's house and its occupants were spared. My Grandmother Clarkes' house was bombed on Chapman Street, but the fan stuck in the roof of the spare bedroom as it came down. Needless to say, it didn't go off and my Uncle Bob, Gran's third husband, (stone deaf and of a kind and simple nature) pulled the bomb out and took it down to the bomb disposal unit down the street, much to the horror of all concerned. It never went off and the ARP dismantled it. The hole it left in the ceiling was there for years; my Gran didn't fix it, but just closed the bedroom door.

My father never stayed in the shelter as he was part of the home guard and captain of the local village unit. The Home Guard (originally called the "Local Defense Volunteers" and later humorously re-named *Look Duck Vanish*) was Britain's last defense against a German invasion and was made up of volunteers. Men like scientists and engineers (my father was an engineer) did not join the forces because their jobs were too important in wartime. Some men were not fit enough to join and they volunteered as fire fighters or ARP (Air Raid Precaution) wardens. They could also join the home guard. Home Guard units had to protect Britain from German parachute attacks.

They kept a lookout for spies, guarded factories, airfields and beaches. Their nickname was "Dad's Army" because many of them were quite old. They sometimes wore tin helmets to protect their heads. In the beginning they had no ammunition, so they carried large broom handles, but later on they received used guns from Canada. Being the Captain of his unit my father had the only good gun issued to his unit and it was a sten gun. He had about eight men in his unit. He told stories of his unit going to a nearby chalk quarry for target practice and listening to his chuckling stories I gather they spent many a lively Sunday afternoon. One of his favourite stories was how on the first practice session, the first man to step up accidentally shot the string that held up the makeshift target. On another occasion, the army battalion that was stationed at the end of the lane in a large field, broadcast they were having an exercise to test the security of their camp. All personnel were warned to be on the lookout for German troops impersonating British civilians or soldiers. Hearing this, my father, ever the practical joker, led his unit to the base with his small unit of four men in a car and four following on foot. The sentry stepped forward with a "Who goes there?" "We have an appointment with the Captain regarding maneuvers of the local Home Guard" replied my father. "Enter" said the guard. Immediately inside the gate the men ran to the various huts and the radio room and broadcast they had seized the camp. The base Captain was furious with my Dad and banned the army's football game with Dad's unit, which had been scheduled for the following week.

During the day my father worked at the dockyard on ships that limped home battle scarred and wounded, repairing and dispatching them back out to sea as soon as possible. In the evening he became a soldier and donning his army outfit and tin hat he went out to patrol the nearby country lanes and beaches.

In 1941, women between the ages 19-30 had to register for war work. All fit young men between the ages of 20 and 22 had to join the navy, army or air force and this age limit was soon changed to include all those 18 to 41. Each street had an Air Raid Warden. Their job was to send for fire engines and ambulances and to check for casualties and unexploded bombs.

During the Blitz approximately two million houses were destroyed and 60,000 civilians were killed. Another 87,000 were seriously injured. The majority of those killed lived in London. Until halfway through the war, more women and children in Britain had been killed than soldiers.

Where people could not have access to a shelter, large trenches were dug in parks and lined with concrete or steel. People would hide in these, as many as fifty people to a trench. In London people hid in the underground railway. In London also, special trains ran every night to Kent, where people went to hide in caves. Music concerts and church services were held in the caves. Tilbury Arch underground station in London was another famous hiding place. The cellars and vaults there could hold around 3,000 people, but on some nights it was estimated 16,000 people went down there. The underground proved not to be as safe as people thought, high explosive bombs could penetrate deep underground. At Marble Arch station 20 people were killed; at Balham, 600 killed, at Bank 111 killed and at Bethnal Green 178 died. Many children were evacuated during the war, some just to the countryside, others were sent abroad. Some of these children were used as child labour and suffered serious abuse in their new homes. Other children stayed in danger areas because their parents refused to have them evacuated. I'm glad I was one of those; my father refused to send me away.

We had gas masks and they were kept in the house. The smell of strong rubber pervaded all your senses when you put them on. There is a picture of my brother and me on Guy Fawkes Night, in which our "Guy" was wearing one of our masks.

Although I was only four when the war ended, many memories were written indelibly into my mind. My heart still sinks if I hear the wail of a siren and watching a movie recently in which a whistle bomb was falling, I actually stopped breathing. When the whistle stopped in the movie, I felt my whole body tense up tightly and when it hit the ground and exploded, I jumped almost out of my seat. After all these years, that whistle put me right back into the shelter. As long as you heard the whistle you were safe because it was still in the air, but when the whistle stopped that was the point you held your breath. We would sit frozen for what felt like an eternity until you heard it explode and realized with guilty relief that it had struck somewhere else. For years after the war I was haunted by them and could never go to bed at night unless my mother came upstairs with me and stood in the bedroom. I checked under the bed every night for "Germans" without even knowing what the word meant. I had nightmares most nights that the dreaded monsters had somehow got under the bed and calling to my parents if I could sleep with them I was doubly mortified when they said I could, but never came to get me. Crossing that floor alone, with the thought that someone was lurking in the room, required much more courage than I possessed and once safely harboured under their covers I made a childish vow to kill myself if anything should ever happen to them.

The steady drone of a Lancaster Bomber is especially haunting. We lived very close to two aerodromes' (Waltham and Binbrook) and every night the Lancaster's would fly over the house in packs on their way out to Europe. I remember specifically one afternoon and long after the war, playing ball at the front of the house, when I heard the drone of a single Lancaster coming over. The familiar buzz caused me to instinctively stop and stare up at the sky, to wait gravely for the plane to pass, when I could resume my solitary game.

There are the conversations I heard also both during the war years and after. I was brought up on the many war songs that were popular at that time; *"White Cliffs of Dover"*, *"Who do you think you're kidding Mr. Hitler?"* *"Happy days are here again."* Vera Lynn sang a lot of the songs. I was named after the song *"Diane."*

Neighbours who owned a car once took me out for a Sunday drive and we went to the nearby aerodrome of Binbrook (home of the famous Dam Busters). They showed me row upon row of bombs stored in sheds with the fans sticking out.

For my parents the war years must have been unbearable. As a child, I had no idea of what was at risk, but they went into that shelter not knowing if they would come out. My father had lots of amusing stories about the war and many were the jokes that ensued about the calamities. Most people made light of it afterwards. But there are some bad stories that occasionally emerge. Such as the time Dad was standing in our back garden during an air - raid and watching a German bomber coming over from the sea. Search lights picked it up and it was brought down, but not before the pilot released a bomb and my father, hearing the swish and hiss as it tumbled over and over above his head, dropped quickly to the ground. The bomb exploded in Joe Lidgards' corn field, at the bottom of the garden. Our back garden was about one hundred yards long, rambling and unkempt it meandered into Joe's field. On another occasion my father was cycling to work in the morning after the nightly raid and picking his way through the ruins of town saw an old man still in his iron bed. The man dead and the bed perched precariously on the edge of a second floor, bared now with walls and windows blown away.

Grimsby was also one of the few places in England that Hitler released thousands of *"Butterfly Bombs."* The Butterfly Bombs, which littered the area, hampered fire-fighting crews attempting to reach locations damaged by the incendiary bombs and the search for them continued for a month after the raid. The raid on the night of June 13, 1943, was a major event in the town's wartime annals, when a large formation of German bombers descended on the town with a vengeance. The raid was a mixture of high explosive, incendiary and anti-personnel bombs known as *SD2*s, aka– the *Butterfly Bomb*. These devices killed indiscriminately. They contained, among other things, nitroglycerine and were fitted with a sophisticated anti-handling device.

Butterfly bombs were first used against Ipswich in 1940, but were also dropped on Grimsby and Cleethorpes in June 1943. The British Government deliberately suppressed news of the damage and disruption caused by butterfly bombs in order not to encourage the Germans to keep using them. They looked like a tin can with wings on. Some were devised to explode as soon as someone picked it up, others were on a timer. Thousands of people were killed by these, especially little children who thought they were toy airplanes. Lots of people picked them up, curious to see what they were. These bombs were dropped on Grimsby and surrounding areas for two nights in a row. My father says he remembers cycling to work and the ground was littered with them, he had the sense not to touch them but cycled around everyone.

RATIONING

One of the ways the war was won was through rationing. Merchant ships were often sunk by the enemy and factory production was concentrated on the war. Lots of things were in short supply. Food was the first thing and I remember taking ration books to the store for many years when buying food. If you bought some sugar, you had to pay for it and give a coupon. If you wanted more sugar and had used up your weeks allotment you had to wait until next week to use another coupon. The government wanted people to try and grow their own vegetables and because of the meat shortage people were encouraged to eat rabbits. Lots of posters were put up in public places that said *"Dig for Victory"* to encourage people to grow their own food. These new laws gave birth to the *"Land Army."* Lots and lots of women worked the land while the men were off to fight. During the war my family hosted a land army woman; she had come from the midlands and stayed with us for a short time.

Rationing was still in effect in 1952, when at the age of eleven years I was on my first ever school trip to York. Waiting for the train at York station to come home, my teacher came up to ask what I had in my bag. I told him I had bought gifts for my brother and sister. He said "What do you have for your Mom and Dad?"

"Nothing, I don't have anything" I replied.
"Come" he said and off we went to the trolley on the station that sold newspapers and candies.
"How about a chocolate bar?" the teacher asked.
"I don't have coupons" I replied.
At that he pulled out his ration book and gave the man some coupons, two I think. We bought a small Cadbury bar of plain chocolate.
I was mortified! The coupons were better than gold and he had just used two!

As soon as I got home I burst into the room and cried excitedly, "Mom, my teacher gave *2 coupons for a chocolate bar, we have to pay him back!*" It was a huge deal to use coupons.

We had powdered eggs and milk, never fresh and many are the meals I had of a bowl of hot milk with dry bread torn into it. I hated milk then and I hate it now! Or having to drink a cup of Bovril and hating it so much I cried all night into it.

There was a famous cartoon going about at the time of a figure with a half-moon head and long nose peering over a brick wall Written on the wall was a slogan that said "Wot! No food" The man on the wall was called "Chad." My father taught me to draw this cartoon and as kids we would always be drawing Chad looking over the wall. We later called our first dog Chad.

The following table shows a weekly allowance for one adult.

Butter: 50g (2oz)	Bacon and ham: 100g (4oz)	Margarine: 100g (4oz)
Sugar: 225g (8oz).	Meat: To the value of **1s.2d** (one shilling and two pence per week.	Milk: 3 pints (1800ml) occasionally dropping to 2 pints (1200ml).
Cheese: 2oz (50g)	Eggs: 1 fresh egg a week.	Tea: 50g (2oz).
Jam: 450g (1lb) every two months.	Dried eggs 1 packet every four weeks.	Sweets: 350g (12oz) every four weeks

Food was rationed for 14 years.

In 1946, when food was just as short as during the preceding years, bread was added to the ration and the sweet ration was halved.

Clothes were also rationed as of June 1941. Everyone had sixty six clothing coupons per year. Clothes made had to use as little material as possible. A man's suit could have only three pockets, no turn ups, three buttons and a maximum length of forty eight cm. A ladies dress could have no elastic waist, no fancy belts. A nightdress would cost six coupons; a man's overcoat cost sixteen coupons, a ladies dress cost eleven coupons, four coupons for underpants and eight coupons for pajamas. Women were encouraged to repair and remake old clothes. Old curtains were cut up and old sweaters were unraveled and re-knitted. My clothes at that time were made by my grandmother. Dresses were made from my father's old shirts and underwear was made from Barrage Balloons (pale yellow). I had lots of white dresses with coloured braid round the hem for decoration. One dress was made from two shirts, a blue check and a white one. The bodice had a large V shape insert of blue check; the skirt was blue check with a broad white hem. My favourite dress of all time was made from a parachute. It was olive green and had short puff sleeves, each sleeve had tiny pink ribbon bows and there was tiny pink lacing up the front bodice. That dress never wore out. The "parachute" dress went through the whole family. Most of my mother's sisters wore it until they got too big, then I got it, then my sister did. I loved that dress and every time I wore it I looked for the highest wall or stairs I could find to jump off. The whole skirt would billow out just like a parachute. Not all hand me-downs were welcome though, I remember with utter horror, my mother insisting I try on a mustard woollen suite that had been my aunts wedding suit. Bear in mind I am an extremely diminutive ten years old, my aunt a well-developed twenty something. This suit had a fitted jacket with huge padded shoulders and a gored skirt. I looked like 'ET' coming out of the closet; all I needed was the blanket over my head. I was totally ridiculous and told my mother so; you couldn't get me in a coffin in that outfit. My father also cobbled our shoes. As soon as we got new shoes he put an extra sole of thick leather on the bottom and studs on the heels so we wouldn't wear them out too fast. My grandmother had tiny wooden clogs made for me as an infant which I loved. My father also built a huge floor loom and wove a lot of material. He made some brown and white tweed which was made into a coat and hat for me. A red and blue check became a coat for my mother; herringbone tweed a suit for my brother. He also wove fine cloth for ties, one was glass fibre but it was awful and irritated your neck in a million places.

An army unit was stationed down the lane in what had been a holiday camp; you could hear the trumpet reveille in the morning. I became the camp mascot according to my mother, as the soldiers stationed there had left families at home or their children were sent away. My mother tells me the soldiers would often pick me up as a baby and take me to the camp for a visit. Every Sunday the regiment would march to church and as I grew older, I would stand at our gate on a Sunday morning waiting for the soldiers and then fall right into line as they marched down the lane. Along the way, a few other children also joined us for we had squatters in some of the deserted homes. My hair would still be in rags because every night my mother put rags in my hair to make ringlets, I tore out the rags as I marched. While the soldiers attended the church service, I played outside in the graveyard. Once or twice I did go in because the church started giving out sticker stamps for attendance with a little booklet to stick them in. I was more interested in getting the stamps than anything else.

I loved it when my grandmother would visit us from town but she always made sure she caught the 4.30p.m. bus home so she could get to her shelter before the raids started. Mom says she was terrified of the nightly raids.

Eventually the war ended and we were returned to a peaceful way of life. The effects lasted a long time however, the bombed buildings did not disappear overnight and neither did ration books and the general state of poverty. It wasn't easy and England was devastated, going into a state of near bankruptcy. People had to pick themselves up, clean up the mess and try to find work again. Many faced terrible injuries; some were homeless or had lost family members.

FAMILY

COUNTRY LIFE

At the age of five, I started school at Peaks Lane Junior School in Humberston and hated every minute of it. After a lot of tears and arguing I persuaded my mother and the headmaster to let me leave and go into town to Bursar Street School. I was much happier there, even though it was a long way to go. We did not have school buses, so I went into town on the regular double decker bus which ran on an hourly schedule. It was a fun rollicking ride of about one hour and then a twenty minute walk to the school. I liked riding on the top deck and the early buses had long wooden seats which ran across the top floor, with the aisle running along the right side of the bus. I always went upstairs, back seat, because we as children wisely realised you got a longer ride at the back! Sometimes if I had company we sat at the very front and would swing our legs absentmindedly up to the front panel. Invariably the bus would come to a sudden halt and the driver came charging upstairs and gave us a big yelling out. He said the sound of our feet on his head was driving him mad. Yet, just as suddenly we forgot his outrage and started swinging our feet again. Then the bus would stop in the middle of nowhere and we realized we were in for it again with nowhere to hide. The drivers and conductors were altogether though a nice bunch and they knew us by name and we knew them. Once, when I came home late in the dark, as I got off at the farmers gate, the driver waited for me to go in front of the bus and let me run in the headlights to our garden gate. That was a great thrill. It was exciting to be running like mad in the middle of a lonely road in the headlights of a huge double decker bus that was creeping ever so slowly behind me.

Life at Humberston was peaceful and quiet. Playmates were scarce and the houses were few and far between. I played mostly alone or with Isobel who lived next door but one. Isobel was older than me and her parents managed the Humberston Golf Course. They were affluent compared to us and came from Dunfermline in Scotland. Isobel wore lovely clothes and once her mother gave me a whole outfit that Isobel and grown out of. It was a hand-made kilt, that had millions of tiny pleats and it swayed when you walked. There was also a yellow botany wool sweater and a blue tweed hacking jacket. I remember wearing that outfit to school once when I had to go to a music exam. I felt like a million dollars in that outfit. Mrs. Ramsey also gave me the pin for the kilt. It was a super kilt and had been made especially for Isobel.

I started piano lessons also at the age of five. My music teacher, Mrs. James, lived on Church Avenue in Humberston. On Saturday mornings I walked to my lesson, a good hour walk. Along North Sea Lane to what is now the Countryman Inn. It was then an old farmhouse with a large pond in front, rumoured to be bottomless. Local lore said there was a horse and cart at the bottom and I was careful never to go near its banks. Instead I crossed a wide cinder track into a little wooded copse. In there a lovely little brook hurried and chattered over tiny pebbles and an old wooden plank served as a small bridge. Clambering up the shallow bank on the far side I climbed over a wooden style. It was like a secret little fairy glade and I loved going into it. Once over and out of the wood, I was in a huge meadow which in the spring was a vast carpet of yellow cowslips. I walked along the hedge the full length of this field to another wooden style, up and over I went then down another cinder track to my teacher's house. Unlatching a tall wooden gate, I walked through her apple orchard, into her vegetable garden, ending up in her flower garden at her back door. After the lessons I was sent out of the front door and in May was given an armful of lily of the valley (my birth flower as Mrs. James always told me). Two huge patches grew by her front door. I walked back a different route, down Church Avenue, to North Sea Lane, past Squire Taylor's house. Squire Taylor's daughter was about sixteen and had long light brown hair which she wore in one long braid down her back. She had a short sturdy build, a heart shape face with rosy cheeks and fine grey eyes. I only ever saw her in jodhpurs and a tweed jacket. Every year she entered in the local gymkhana with her pony. Their house was a large red brick mansion with ivy creeping up the walls; it had a large forecourt of crushed gravel and a sweeping circular driveway. A high brick wall surrounded the extensive property with two large black iron gates. I would press my cheeks through the railing and stare in wonder at the grandeur, admiring the big red brick house with its many windows and manicured gardens.

By stark contrast and across from the squire was Joe Lidgards' thatched cottage. The cottage, nestled in a bright little garden, was small and made of white stucco with tiny lattice windows and a tremendous thatched roof. Joe Lidgard was the local farmer and owned most of the surrounding farmland. He also had several head of cattle and one serious looking bull. He worked hard on the land every day. Sometimes Joe would be driving his cows up the road as I was walking home. Terrified of the large clumsy looking animals I hid in the hedge until they had gone past. From the thatched cottage I continued up the rise and past the bottomless pond again. It was a lovely walk and I sometimes talked to the birds or sang. I especially liked the little brook that gurgled through my secret wood and the blaze of yellow cowslips in the spring. Once, at the top of the rise, an old lady came running to her garden gate on seeing me limping badly, "Come in" she said and I did. This kind old sole sat me in a wide comfy arm chair, made me a cup of tea, took off my ill-fitting shoes and applied corn plasters to my toes. Ah what heaven it was when I put the cruel shoes back on! I will never forget her kindness.

The village of Humberston had many lovely wild flowers, yellow kingcups, broad white daisies that could be woven into a necklace or bracelet, carpets of bluebells, pink wild roses in the hedgerows, purple and white clover which you sucked for the juice from the buds, buttercups, to shine under your chin that told you if you liked butter.

Although we lived a very modest life, there was untold richness to our tapestry of days. Wide open spaces to roam, haystacks to roll in, a long beach with tidal pools of warm water for tiny feet and in the evenings when my father was home, the radio. My father would tune the little brown box on a Sunday night to radio Luxemburg for the *"Ovaltinies"* a weekly show for children. There were stories and competitions and memberships. Each program ended with a secret coded message. In order to know the code you had to be a member and I was particularly chagrined that I was not. Telling me not to worry about it, my father moved to the table and listening to the secret message began to write on a small piece of paper. I watched captivated as he slowly and with furrowed brow, studied the strange code, then scribbling furiously he looked up smiling broadly and handed me the note. Voila! Here was the secret message. It was magical to know I had got the secret without being a member and I swelled with pride that my father was the cleverest person on earth. Looking back now, I have to smile and wonder if he really was such a great code-breaker, or a kind imposter. Other nights he tuned into a pirate offshore station called Hilversum. This was always Scottish music and for this we pushed all the furniture up against the wall in our small back living room. We three children then performed Highland flings as had been taught to us, arms held high, perfectly pointed toes and careful not to touch the pretend swords crossed under our feet. Mother and father watched and cheered as we danced until we could dance no longer, falling about laughing and breathless. The bleak house momentarily lit up with the sound of music and gaiety, its occupants savouring the moment, careless of the world and its troubles.

TODAY I AM BABYSITTING

Today I am baby-sitting Liam, (Nick and Josee have gone to a funeral) and Liam and I have renewed our acquaintanceship nicely. I sat him in a Blue Box and pushed him crashing into walls and furniture; he loved it, squealing with delight the whole time. As I count to three for the take-off he says "two?" Then each time we crashed; beautiful big brown eyes looked up to me questioningly and two perfect rosebud lips formed the word "TWO?"

At night Liam is positively exasperated that my Abyssinian cat will not come to bed and sleep with him. "But Pasha, we laaave u" he pleads and paying homage to his Italian heritage, thrusts out a miniature embrace. Pasha merely blinks and walks away with cool military dignity. He has been manhandled by this being before and does not intend to go through with it again. However, the early morning sun finds a purring ball of fur at the foot of the bed and Liam jumps up at the ready. "Come" says a gentle child voice and out go the loving arms again. "Come, come" he coaxes again and again. Pasha stirs and looks on impassively. "You will have no egeny in the morning" comes a now louder child speak. I am watching this entertaining scene from my pretend sleep. Pasha is seriously testing the patient waters of a not - quite - two- year old and Liam is coming to the end of it. The shore of frustration is finally reached and abruptly throwing tiny arms up in despair, a very loud child voice scolds, "Pasha! I'm tired of these silly games."

January 4ᵗʰ 1998

22

ELIZA ANN STORY, aka daddymam

Smelling of "lily of the valley" and sucking on a 'mint imperial,' her ample frame was a cushioned embrace. An oval face with high cheekbones had small wistful blue eyes. Short and thinning silver hair was coaxed into random kiss-curls on a high forehead, long gold ear-rings dangled from perfect ears. She was short, round and soft. Her hugs were like falling into a warm cosy armchair. Lovable and loved, she was our grandmother.

Gran lived in row housing, known locally as the 'back streets' of Grimsby. The house was just one of many such identical homes on what was known as the West Marsh of Grimsby. Now don't start imaging some wild rural grassy marsh with plants, reeds and all varieties of water species. No my friend, this was a concrete sprawl of row upon row of terrace houses. The houses were old and worn, built in the 1800's of dark red bricks, with slate roofs and two sash windows, one up and one down. These particular houses were built on leased land, a ninety nine years lease whose time was up.

It's a mystery why a child would love to be there as opposed to the large garden and fresh air of our own country living, but I did love staying there. The house had no toys; there was no garden to play in, nothing in fact that held any special attraction for active child minds, but it had love, it was a contented place.

The long bi-weekly journey to visit my grandmother from our house by the sea took about one hour on each of two double decker buses and then a good twenty minute walk up Corporation Road, assuming the big iron lift bridge was down. Sometimes the bridge was up to allow a trawler up the river, stopping both traffic and pedestrians. When the bridge was down we loitered anyway to catch sight of the white lucent jelly fish swimming just below the surface of the murky waters below. As we rounded the corner onto Chapman Street, sometimes, if he was not at sea, Uncle Bob would be standing on the doorstep. We would see his head peering out and then suddenly it would vanish, only to re-appear again. This was my uncle running in to tell my Gran we were coming, at which she fast-tracked into the kitchen to put the chip pan on to make us a big batch of chips, almost ready to eat when we arrived at her door.

Dark and dank inside, you entered directly off the street, through a heavy wooden door. Going down the dark narrow hallway you were confronted by a long steep staircase at its far end. A door on your right led to the front parlour, seldom used except when Gran was at her sewing machine, an old singer treadle. The machine sat right in front of the window, not only for the extra light it afforded, but allowing Gran to see who was walking by on the street. Their footsteps were audible as they approached and faded away, as were the conversations. The room was crammed with large furniture and the walls and mantle piece were cluttered with antique clocks and all manner of antique bric-a-brac.

The next and last room from the hallway was the living room. A small room besieged again with large pieces of furniture. Immediately inside the door you were confronted by a large square table, it hugged the wall and was covered in a red chenille tablecloth. A large lumpy sofa was pushed up against one side of the table, so that on the rare occasion someone sat here to eat, they had to sit on the arm of the sofa. The far side of the table was also home to another equally large and lumpy armchair, inviting any future diner to sit on its wide and beckoning arm. A large black hob fireplace dominated the opposite wall. Under the narrow window, which looked out onto the back yard, sat a small radio on a low table, in later years a small television was added. Behind the sofa and facing the large hob fireplace was a large white hutch with stain glass windows. Inside the hutch was dry foods such as sugar, tea, etc. and cookies, which we called biscuits. The bottom part had solid doors and was always locked. These cupboards stored a score of assorted treasures. Beyond this room and at the back of the house was the scullery and pantry. The scullery had a red tile floor, a gas stove sitting on the left in an alcove and underneath a narrow sash window on the right, a large porcelain sink and wooden draining board. There was also a wringer washer machine. The walk-in pantry was large and had long white wooden shelves that went up to the ceiling. On one bottom shelf sat a small meat safe that had a mesh door. A basin held fresh eggs in the days when gran kept chickens. Outside from the kitchen door you entered a very small flagstone courtyard which was enclosed by a looming brick wall that hid the neighbours next door. Going away from the house and at the end of the small yard was a coal house and then the outside toilet, with its wide wooden bench seat, long chain handle flush and a nail on the wall holding squares of freshly torn newspaper. There was an abandoned garden beyond a high wooden trellis gate and beyond that the brick alley that ran behind the houses.

Needless to say, trips to the outhouse were the only reason to go out the back door. Every house was identical in design and build and inhabited mainly by working class people, mostly fishermen or dock labourers. There were deckhands, as my grans husband was, wireless operators, cooks, lumpers and the likes. Since Grimsby at that time was the world's largest fishing port, most people worked for the industry in one capacity or another.

The street was one of many that ran perpendicular on both sides from the main road of Corporation Road. Chapman street was cut into two sections by a cross street. On the corners at this intersection was a beer store; commonly known as an 'off-licence,' *Lashbrooks*, (a small grocery store), a candy store and on the fourth corner, a saw mill.

On Sundays, gran always cooked a roast of beef and a batch of large Yorkshire puddings, which was served as a first course with onion gravy. I was sent to the corner off-licence with a big blue and white porcelain jug for a pint of bitter which we drank at dinner. The whole thing was delicious and I ate it greedily from the fat cushiony arm of the sofa. Mornings were just as homey. I would wake in the deep feather bed to the sound of the mill starting up. After quickly dressing, Gran gave me money to go over to *Lashbrooks* for a 'shilling cob.' This was a round cob of freshly baked bread, still warm from the oven. I cut huge, inch thick slices and smothered them with butter and lemon curd, washing it all down with a large mug of tea. The big black kettle whistled on the hob and the coal embers cast a warm rosy glow over the room, even in summertime.

About ten o'clock we would go shopping. Down the street gran waddled, shopping bag in hand and I skipping gaily at her side. Our first stop was the 'Meadow' a grocery store. It consisted of one large room that had shelves all around stocked with tins and packages. A set of scales sat atop a large wooden counter by the door. On the floor were sacks of sugar and flour. On the counter, a huge slab of deep yellow butter sat waiting to be molded into neat little cubes. Gran bought sugar, which was carefully weighed on the scale then scooped into a small blue paper bag, next was butter which was cut and patted into a neat little square with wide wooden paddles. This was wrapped carefully into wax paper. All these were deposited into the basket she carried. Now we cross the road for some meat for dinner. "Morning Liza" says the butcher. He has a large white apron which is stained with blood; it's cool in here and stark. There are slabs of meat under a glass counter and sausages and there is a faint savoury smell. We are buying "penny ducks" also known as faggots. Gran buys them a lot; they are enormously delicious and will be smothered in thick gravy at dinnertime. Next it's to Gooseman the chemist; he is almost like a doctor. People sit in the tight little shop and wait their turn to tell Gooseman their ailment. Dressed in his long white coat, bespectacled and slightly bald, he is a quiet serious man who takes great care of his patrons. Without any fuss, he quietly disappears behind his high counter to mix magic potions to dispense. Next we go much further down the road to goodie Taylors. This is a sweet shop, but we call it the goodie shop. Gran always buys a quarter pound of mint imperials. I vary my selection often. The shop is surrounded by shelves upon shelves of big glass jars, each filled to the brim with goodies. The choice is dizzying, as I cast my eyes along the rows. What will I have today; humbugs, pear drops, Tom Thumb drops, lemon sherbets, liquorice allsorts, toffees, caramels, or dolly mixtures? I don't mind at all having to work hard on a decision, I am completely up to the job. Our shopping all done, we drift home, perhaps gran will stop at the bookies. She loves to gamble on the horse races. If we don't, we will go straight home and she will check the radio or read the newspaper to see where her bets are to go and I will be sent down the street again. Knocking on the door of a house in the alley and handing over coins wrapped in paper, I will declare loudly "Two and six on X, each way, thank you." then turning abruptly, walk away with a smug feeling of having done something very adult.

Needless to say, my parents take a very dim view of these events. My mother is especially horrified at my flea bites from the feather bed. Even worse, they find out I have been some times parked on the steps of the Kings Arms pub while Gran goes in for a quick pint. I haven't told them that sometimes I am sneaked in and sit behind my grans ample frame in the dark corners of the booth.

Still, despite these hiccups, I am still able to get my overnight vacations. As I get older and enter my teen years, these visits turn into independent regular day excursions. We have also moved much closer now, living in town. Later still, at the age of seventeen, I will live with gran when my parents and siblings move back to live in Canada. I have refused to go this time, but will stay behind with my boyfriend Roy and follow them in a year or so as Roy's apprenticeship ends.

I have no problem living with my grandmother; in fact, I love it, despite the condition of the house, which is now close to its demolition date. Because this house is on the dock side of town and probably was once a marsh, it is exceedingly damp. The large wooden door has swollen and to open from the outside one has to give a good strong biff with the shoulder. Similarly, once inside, a good kick with your foot will ensure it is closed. These actions each cause the big brass knocker to bang loudly. As the North Sea Tide rises, the walls are actually wet to a height level with the top of the dining table and if you come in at night, you learn to stand still as a statue after you turn the hall light on. Large blackcock beetles will go running along the carpet back under the base boards. The worn and threadbare carpets also bear silver streaks of slug trails, nightly crawlers, while we slept upstairs in the soft cloud of a feather bed. But one luxury that my father has insisted on before leaving for Canada, an inside toilet and the pantry behind the scullery has been turned into a pristine flush toilet. Now at least I do not have to navigate the dismal outside brick yard or use a chamber pot in the bedroom at night. I am happy living with my gran anyway, we have an understanding. She loves the company too and cooks me a supper which is ready for me every night when I come home from work. In strawberry season she buys me a pint of my favourite fruit every day and I eat it all. In the evenings, Roy comes to visit on his motorcycle. These narrow streets are like boom-boxes and I can hear the bike way up on Corporation Road. As it turns onto Chapman Street, its motor growls louder and louder with each doorway achieved. Finally coming to a snarling stop at my grans door, there is a moment of silence, then a hefty shoulder pushes the door open, clang goes the knocker and then a heavy motorcycle boot kicks the door shut, the brass knocker protests loudly again. The soft spoken neighbour who lives on our right, tells my grandmother that when she hears the first whines of the bike on Corporation Road, she turns to her husband and says, "Hang on father!" as the nightly ritual of Roy making his grand entrance begins.

Interesting characters live around us; next door are the afore-mentioned quiet and tidy couple who have one son, on our left are the family Delatouch. Anne is the matriarch, short and stout, with short frizzed red hair, she is a workaholic. Her husband is a wireless operator on the trawlers; he is rarely at home, but out at sea for weeks at a time. Anne rules her brood of five children with an iron fist. She works constantly; her house is stark and minimally furnished. The hob is well oiled, the fire always neat, the table top bare and scrubbed white, out in the yard the washing is hanging. I have never seen Anne smile, she goes about her duties seriously, on hands and knees, scrubbing her front step so white that you don't want to step on it, but carefully jump over. She hangs out of bedroom windows washing the sashes and walks to the shops every day for fresh meat for dinner. Her house smells of soap.

Across the road live the McVarney's. They seem poor. There is a father, who I have not seen, a mother who stands untidily on her front steps. There is a daughter who sometimes stands on the step with her. Maureen is in her teens, uncombed stringy brown hair hangs limply around an oblong forlorn looking face. There seems to be troubles in this home and I feel sad when I look at Maureen.

Every Sunday, the Salvation Army marches down the street, going first to the end, where they form a circle and proceed to play, after about half an hour, they move up and form another circle right outside of our door. From the bedroom window I watch transfixed at the uniformed men and women, the big brass drum and the bold trumpets. A lady in a suit and fancy bonnet will leave the circle and knock on all the doors, asking for a donation.

There's a boy with a wooden barrow who comes along; he has comics and newspapers. We buy four comics every week; the *Dandy*, the *Beano*, the *Film Fun* and the *Radio Stars*; gran has the *News of the World*, which is full of scandal. I with a big mug of tea and gran with a mug of Guinness, spend Sunday in idle cosy reading.

Gran is married a second time, but Uncle Bob is also usually at sea, he is a deck-hand. The trawlers are deep ocean netters and go to Iceland and the Faroe isles. There is a movie produced in Grimsby of the harsh life of these fishermen at sea, it is called *"Out with the tide"* and I have a copy of it at home. It is filmed largely at sea where men and boat are mere specs on an angry sea, where ice is so thick it has to be chipped off the rigging and there in the last few frames, is Uncle Bob, standing on that frozen deck and grinning alongside the other crew. He never once talked of the rough days he spent out on the cruel North Sea.

The bulldozers were on the street and finally they came to number eighty. Still refusing to leave, my Gran sat stubbornly on the old lumpy sofa staring into the big black fireplace. My father stood at her side, "it's no use" he said, "You simply have to go."

That night I went to visit my gran in her brand new shiny bungalow. It was situated on a rise above one of the busiest roads in town. Gone were the neighbours of old, the Salvation Army band and the newsboy with his wooden barrel. Gone was the 'bookie' at the end of the street. My father had dragged out the old sofa and chair but nothing else. Roy and I hurried back to the old house to retrieve as much of the past as we could. The house was boarded up and we had to enter by the long back alley up to her back door, now smashed in. Inside was a scene of complete devastation. Cupboards and drawers had been upended in the middle of the floor, gone were the Victorian silhouettes on the wall, the bronze Greek 'Discus thrower' and 'Thinker' from the mantelpiece and not a single antique wall clock was left. Gran was an avid collector of clocks and whiled away many hours, taking apart, fixing and oiling them. She'd had a total of thirteen wall clocks in the front room and many an antique dealer had knocked on the door asking for a trade, her collection had been well known.

The house was dead, lying bare and stripped of its former life, no sound to be heard but the dripping of a leaking tap. It was a wretched sight and closed the chapter on a way of life that had been rich and large and the likes of which would not be seen again.

THE DESERT SONG

Christmas; it is the season of sharing and giving, peace and joy; a time to be with those we love and cherish. But for many it is very much a difficult season, the homeless, the sick, the lonely, or the poor. As I approach this season, I am watching my mother struggle to keep a brave face as her first Christmas without her lifelong companion draws near. It brings back memories too for me of my father and I got to thinking of the visits to him we paid this year in the Brant Centre, a long term facility in Burlington where he spent his last few months and days.

The visits were not usually happy occasions. Sunk into depression, with legs that would not walk, ears that could not hear and a mind that could not compute, my father only wanted to lie in bed and sleep.

On one such occasion, my mother and I insisted he get up and putting him in his wheelchair, we wheeled a reluctant man down the hall. Taking him to one of the common rooms, it was hard work to ignite any spark of interest. Pictures in my camera of grandchildren and great grandchildren brought momentary flashes of real joy, but then he soon became far away again and asked only to go back to bed. "Shall we play cards?" I asked. "No" replied my father quietly. Of course not, he cannot remember how to play and quickly becomes upset. "How about watching TV?" I try again. But this will not work either, his eyesight is bad and in any case, he doesn't understand it anymore.

It can be very tiring trying to entertain an Alzheimer patient. Searching for something, I suddenly came upon a bright idea. "Why not play the piano Dad?" I said. He had always been a great pianist, never needing music; you know one of those people who can play anything 'by ear.' "No", he frowned. "I can't play anymore." "But you can" I enthused, "you just need to practice." So flush with this new energy, I wheeled him tout suite to the music room and parked him in front of the piano. "Go ahead" I urged, "Play something." Slowly and deliberately with one hand and one finger he thumped out....... diddle um dum dum diddle um dum dum. "No" he said, turning away dejectedly, "I cannot." "Then can I play for you?" I pleaded and my father stared back vacantly. I sat down to play, but unlike my father, I need sheet music, so searching through the piano stool I saw a piece called *The Desert Song*. Now this struck me as quite a strange coincidence, as in my younger years when we lived in the country, our neighbour, Mrs. Finch, would sometimes invite me to her home to play her piano. I would be about nine years old at the time and this was a great privilege to sit in her best room, which was usually sealed off to all and sundry. Sitting at her piano I would leaf through her music and play to my heart's content. One of my favourite pieces was from the musical, *"The Student Prince,"* and I especially loved a piece called *"The Desert Song" By Sigmund Romberg*. How strange I thought, that this piece would be sitting there. I whipped out the music sheet with much relish and proceeded to play on this very very old piano. Immediately two budgies atop the piano started to jump around the cage, singing and chirping with great gusto, it was obvious they knew the piece well and sang out lustily. This amused my dad and he beamed at the two songsters. But suddenly from nowhere, they were joined by a strong contralto voice. A voice so strong and pure, that hit every note and sang so clear: *"Blue heavens and you and I and stars kissing a moonlight sky, A desert breeze whispers a lullaby, only stars above us to see I love you!"* The voice was so expressive and beautiful I almost froze, but dared not to stop. I played on, all the while trying to figure out who could this be? I was not aware a singer had been brought in, as sometime they are for a sing-a-long, neither dare I stop to turn around. I played on through the song and chorus and all the time the voice behind me sang out strong and clear, in such perfect tone that I felt a shiver run through my spine. At last the song ended and I was able to turn around. What met my eyes was astonishing, the tiniest and frailest of ladies propped into a wheelchair. Apart from a few residents in the doorway I saw no one else, so this must be 'the voice.' "You have such a beautiful voice" I gasped. "Yes" was the shy and quiet reply, "I used to be a singer." Not wanting to lose the magic I quickly delved into the stool again and produced more music. "Do you know this?" I pointed. Hazel knew them all and if she didn't, she wheeled up closer to the piano and sang the written words to each new song. Always, in this clear strong voice that never missed a note. I don't know how long we played, only that my father sat completely engrossed and several nurses came in to say "Hazel you have a lovely voice, we had no idea!" Absorbed in the music, we almost missed the dinner hour and reluctantly folded up the piano. The birds went back to their silent perches and Hazel and my father were wheeled into the dining room. They shared the same table and as my mother and I left to go home, we peeped in at the window to see the two sitting in animated conversation with an energy and vitality I have not seen in my father for an age.

So the moral of this story is; you definitely don't judge the proverbial book by its cover. All over the world, there are some wonderful people residing in that lonely no man's land called Alzheimer, who have wonderful stories and talents of which we know nothing. And as we gather round our Christmas table with those we love, let us not forget the vacant chairs, the Hazels and the Ronald's of this world, not quite with us but struggling in a different world from which there is no escape. My father never did practise the piano again, but we did have one more concert courtesy of Hazel before my father died.

After silence, that which comes nearest to expressing the inexpressible is music.

Aldous Huxley

THE WHALE

My father once told me I read too much. It's true; I was and still
am an avid reader. I frequented the school library for anything
I could find; *Cinderella, Famous Five adventures, The Secret
Seven, Susanna of the Mounties, Rebecca of Sunnybrook Farm,
What Katy Did, White Boots,* all were captivating and inspiring.
I even started a 'Secret Seven club' in the shed at the bottom of
our garden, we had secret meetings and old pop bottle tops for
badges.

I think I was probably going on ten years old when I heard a
story about a whale that had become beached on the North Sea
shore. Local media described its condition as grave, seemingly
depressed and lonely. A request was made for a volunteer to
go and sit with the whale each day, to soothe, sing and talk
to it. Of course, I thought that was my perfect vocation. I had
heroic dreams of sitting by the side of the Cleethorpes bathing
pool, strumming a guitar and crooning softly to a gigantic black
whale. The fact that I was ten years old, did not own a guitar,
much less could play one, did not matter to me at all, mere minor
details when you are a dreamer. Of course, I didn't get there, but
someone apparently did and despite all efforts, the whale died.

For many years after I often thought about that naive dream of
saving the whale. Time passed, I married and began raising two
small children. One morning, in a sudden bolt of inspiration,
I had the bright idea of buying a guitar. Enrolling in the local
night school I proceeded to struggle through classes of classical
guitar. Frustrated with an exercise one day, I started to chord
simple nursery songs for the entertainment of my two toddlers.
This instantly became a hit and very soon we were our own little
band. Marcelline at half past two was given a tambourine and
Nicholas at four years a recorder. Our collection of songs grew
by the dozens and the concerts became an almost daily habit.

Neighbourhood children sometimes joined our sessions and we thronged to a chorus of lusty infant voices, tambourines, wooden spoons and saucepans. We acted out musical plays with a cast of actors readily available from our regular little gang of street tykes. "A handsome Prince came riding by" sang the chorus, as Nicholas (pretending to be on horseback) came galloping into the living room, twice round the dining table and over to the piano, where I was playing. The "Princess Marcelline" stood in eager anticipation of gallant rescue, while a chorus of knights and ladies-in-waiting, cheered, snapped tambourines and banged cooking pans with wooden spoons.

Those waifs are all now grown with children of their own, but the seed of music was planted. Both Nicholas and Marcelline, mature parents themselves, join me now in piano duets. It is a source of eternal joy to visit my son or daughter and fall into the tradition of making music together. Granddaughters sing at microphones, grandsons and husbands play drums and guitars, we laugh in the joy of sharing these hastily put together performances. Sometimes we take turns at the piano, where tiny fingers plonk out one note stanzas of a duet, while I play the teacher part. Often now, the parents, those same little ones I taught, take the lead and watching them, I am happily reminded of scenes from another time, another place. We have come full circle.

True, our music is not to communicate with a whale, but our message to one another is the same. Sharing, bonding, nurturing, we give our souls flight.

"Music is a moral law. It gives soul to the universe, wings to the mind, flight to the imagination and charm and gaiety to life and to everything." Plato

THE TIES THAT BIND

Marcelline, Evan and Rachel were here February 29th to March 4th. It was a lovely visit, Rachel especially enjoyed herself and as her mom was packing the car to leave, sat on her little rocking chair with a gloomy face and told me:-
"I knew this would happen."
"What?" I asked.
"The sad thing" she replied, "going home."

March 22nd, 2006

THE CHANGING SEA

I was raised on the north east coast of England. We lived in a featureless two storey brick house that sat defiantly by the wind-swept shores of the North Sea. The house, *Devonia* was one in a row of eight lonely houses, which stared out blankly from the surrounding fields, on this last open stretch of the North Sea Lane. The village name was Humberston and the nearest town of Cleethorpes was an hour away by double decker bus. After arriving from town, the bus would sit at the shoreline for a break before its return run into town. Going to school in the morning, you could see if the bus was on the move, making us run a race with it to the designated stop by the gate at Joe Lidgards corn field. In spring there were fields of yellow cowslips and woods with carpets of blue bells and in summer fields of corn, meadows of grazing cows. Summer brought holiday makers (trippers) who came from the midlands to the holiday camps at the end of the lane. But in winter it was remote and harsh. An angry North Sea gale raced up from the shore, howling and moaning around the house, rattling the windows, slamming wooden shutters and giving the doors a good biffing before racing off through the fields and hedges. In the pitch black of night shutters banged, owls screeched and one especially windy night, a runaway horse ran mad circuits around the house before galloping back onto the road.

The long sandy beach, with its dunes and coarse grass was my playground in the summer, but on my way to the shore I browsed the bus stop, picking up used bus tickets. These I traded at school, for they were the size and shape of cigarette cards and had different colours depending on the fare. A sixpenny ticket was a valuable trade for its fare price was the highest and here by the shore they were plentiful. At the sea I collected sea shells, built sand castles and paddled in the cold salty waters while trying in vain to avoid sea weed, crabs and jelly fish.

The North Sea is not friendly, its cold tides are moody and strong and they creep in stealthily by a network of low channels that resemble icy fingers, ready to grasp an innocent wanderer not paying attention. Happily absorbed it can be easy to be caught unawares as many have been. One year a tragic accident brought death to a group of horses and their riders. In 1969, one of the horses, named Candy, became an unlikely local hero. A party of riders had gone for a gallop on the beach when a fog rolled in, dis-orienting the group, the cunning sea sneaked in and trapped them. Candy alone swam to safety, all the way from Cleethorpes to Grimsby docks, where he was rescued. All of the others, horses and riders were lost.

Out on the horizon ships and crew are at the seas mercy, even the carousel at Cleethorpes was fair game when the sea decided to send it piece by piece down to our dunes. On weekends my father loved to comb the beaches with his friend Albert. Together they would bring back the flotsam and jetsam flung there by the snarling morning tide. I remember him bringing us an electric kettle and crates of oranges and grapefruits. The fruit was covered in oil and the two men meticulously washed them in preparation to be sold, since fruit at that time was scarce and they could fetch a good price. The wooden horses from the carousel he left behind.

Our family lived there for eleven years and it was to be the longest place we ever stayed. While I was busy building castles in the sand, my father was building castles in the air. Like the dark and lonely sea, his was a restless and brooding soul. Years of moving and removing began. First we moved back to town, then in a terrifying leap to Canada as emigrants. Of all our moves, this one was to cause the most pain and exact the highest price. As the eldest of three children I was warned to set an example and not to make a fuss or cry. But in the sanctity of my bed at night, I luxuriated in the deep sobs of inconsolable grief. To move to a new country, leaving behind all that was dear and familiar was to me a disaster. Leaving my best friend Roy was bad enough, but to then leave my grandmother was more than I could bear and at the very end could not bring myself to visit her for a last farewell. I simply went away, saving us both from a scene too terrible to imagine.

Our new life in Canada was a shock to my every sense. The big skies, the broad highways, the never-ending forest of trees, even the food tasted different. "Oh children soon adapt" I heard too often. Like jumping free-fall, it is so very hard to let go of what you know and trust and in the dizzying drop down you are never sure how you are going to land. My father moved again and again, always building on a shifting sand, he became a rolling stone, restless as the North Sea waves.

Starting life over in a strange country where we knew absolutely no one took great courage, humility and blind faith. These qualities my father had in spades, I didn't have so much.

Long years have not erased the memory of that painful break. Now, some fifty years later, life has settled down. My brother, sister and I live steady happy lives in this new country, my father also. Aged and frail and bound by ill health he is no longer able to roam. Visiting my parents in their small apartment, I catch my father in a daydream. "Where are you Dad?" I shout. Broken from his reverie he smiles "I am far away" he says," I have been gone miles." "Come back, come back!" I warn, but he is gone again. Sifting through the sands of time he travels backwards, searching for something he cannot find. He has left his heart on the North Sea Shore.

THE SHOEBOX

The best treat you could give me as a child was to send me to my Grandmother's house for a sleepover. It was wonderful to sink into her deep feather bed, read comics and drink cups of tea. Of an evening we would sit in front of a crackling fire listening to the radio, there was no such thing as television then. She taught me how to knit while we listened to scary murder plays. Sometimes Gran would give me a key to her cupboard behind the sofa. The tall white cupboard with its glass doors held biscuits (cookies) sugar, teas etc., but the bottom doors were an absolute treasure trove of gifts. Therein sat new towels and linen table cloths; scented bars of soap and a pair of ruby red slippers. The slippers were made of velvet with Cuban heels and a deep rim of red fur around the ankle. They were the most beautiful slippers I had ever seen and I was allowed to stomp around in them for just a minute before they were safely stowed again. Gran considered all of these items far too pretty to be used. But the most precious item in the cupboard to me was an old white shoebox. This I carried carefully to the sofa where together we poured over its contents. It served as a jewellery box and was filled with all manner of more tiny boxes. Little ring boxes, matchboxes stuffed with clouds of cotton wool that covered tiny ear rings or broaches. As each box was opened, there was a story. "This was your great-grandmothers" "I bought this at the Festival of Britain" "This is a coronation broach from 1953" "Here is a garnet broach with a lock of Aunt Lucy's hair." I was enthralled each time we went through the old shoebox.

When my grandmother died I went to her little bungalow so strange now without her strong presence. My grandfather nodded to a picture of myself on her mantle above the fire "There was the apple of her eye" he mumbled and crossing the room to the cupboard he turned and thrust the shoebox into my hands.

The shoebox sat in my cupboard for several years. I could not bring myself to open it again and left it just as my grandmother had last touched it, afraid that by opening it her essence might somehow evaporate and be lost forever. Some people say that they have communicated with the dead, talked to them and even seen them in a vision. I tried at times to summon my grandmother, talked to her, willed her to appear, but always there was silence and a vacant space.

Last year, Rachel, my four year old grand-daughter came to visit for a weekend. These visits were extremely rare, since they live far away. Elated to be at Grandma's house, she rushed into every room. Exploring every corner and cupboard, she seized upon a glass dish on the coffee table. "I knew you'd have candies" she exclaimed and pushed a large fruit drop into her tiny mouth. At bedtime she insisted on sleeping with Grandma in "her big bed." Rushing about the room in uncontained excitement she again explored drawers and cupboards and there it was the shoe box. "What's this Grandma?" she asked.
"Oh, that is your great grandma's jewellery box"
"Can I see" said an inquisitive little face.
It was difficult to explain to such an innocent request that I did not like to open the box, so I told her to bring me the box.
Snuggling under a large down quilt and propped up by plump pillows, we opened the box.
One by one a tiny hand explored each little box within a box. And I found myself telling the old favourite stories.
"Oh these are beeeaaautiful!" she gasped.
Suddenly as if stabbed, my heart began to race, a tear pricked my eyes and a fear rose in my chest. Oh, I'm surely not going to cry. I cannot cry. I panicked, for suddenly I saw another little girl; a little girl with the same black hair and dark brown eyes, sitting on a lumpy sofa in front of a crackling fire saying "Oh these are beautiful Gran." And there in this room, my grandmother, a presence felt and not seen. She was smiling and she was watching in happy approval at this cycle repeated.

Keeping the lid on the box and hiding it away, I had also hidden my grandmother away. Like rubbing the magic lantern, by opening the lid I had allowed her spirit to rise out into the light. Death feels dark and frightening, but we should not fear it, nor carry our grief jealously like some kind of badge. We must celebrate the life of those we love and give thanks for their presence. Sharing the shoebox has been a welcome release of sad pangs and now two other grand-daughters, Clara and Emma come often to sift through these relics of the past. After all, a treasure shared is a treasure doubled.

BUTTERCUP

She is a tiny wishbone of a figure, delicate, light as a feather. Her fine black hair is long on her shoulders with wispy bangs that fall carelessly over her eyes. Her small round face is full of childish anticipation; long black lashes lay upon dark brown eyes. The button nose, perfect cherry lips and pale rose cheeks, would flatter the most discerning china doll. She is my granddaughter Rachel, a bright slender flower, I call her Buttercup.

Just six years old she mirrors my love for dance and music. From earliest infancy she has sung the alphabet song in perfect pitch. She is bright and was an early talker. Now, as she sings to me her latest number, I am awe struck at the moves, the struts, the swaying hips. "Let's Rock, let's rock" she bellows, flashing a tiny fist into the air.

Her laugh is a squeal, then a tiny ripple, like the sound of a brook gurgling happily on its way.

At bed-time she is swallowed up in the story of "*My Naughty Little Sister*" and empathizes dolefully as she compares "Bad Harry" to her own infant brother Evan, the bane of her short life. Today we go to the ceramic store and pick out various figurines to paint and polish. Rachel has a bear for her Grandpa and a "beautiful" star shaped dish for herself. She takes a long time to paint them, painstakingly dipping the brush into the water, then dabbing again in a bright blue pot of paint, she strikes boldly across the star. I am painting too and now and then she looks up through wisps of straggling black hair and says "Good job Grandma."

On the way home I have found at the ice-cream parlour a counter full of chocolate truffles. While licking huge cones of Rainbow ice cream we eye them hungrily. "Let's buy some" I offer and

Rachel is excited. Together we pick out seven truffles. "It's our secret" I say, "Tonight when everyone goes to bed they will find one on their pillow." Rachel's eyes open wide and a smile as big as the moon creeps over the tiny face. Bed-time now cannot come too soon and she climbs over the sofa to whisper in my ear "Is it time yet Grandma?" I nod yes and we sneak out of the room. Taking a box of Kleenex from her room she tip-toes from room to room. Carefully wrapping each truffle with a tissue, she lays one on each pillow as if it were a fragile petal. She is pleased with the effort, but now wants everyone to go to bed, she wants them all to come and look. "Oh my!" sigh Mom and Dad, "What's this?" "It's a surprise, it's a surprise!" she squeals, jumping up and down and squeezing tiny porcelain hands to her chest.

And now as I tuck her in for the night, a tiny face with a bulging cheek, smiles sleepily from a deep pillow and says, "These caramel one's are really good Grandma."

CAMPING WITH GRANDMA

Richie and I, well into our retirement years, decided that after years of sleeping in tents or under the stars, a motor home would be the new senior way to commune with nature. We became the proud owners of a, 'memories of the seventies,' 1972 Dodge motorhome. We picked up three grandchildren, who were going to help us christen Dora the Dodge and as we drove home I regaled them with preparatory plans for the coming weekend in Algonquin Park.

It was a late Friday afternoon, time was limited, last minute park reservations had not been possible, so a matter of 'first come, first served' lent an air of urgency to our journey home. My precious cargo of three grandchildren, Liam, Clara and Emma at age 16;13;and 12... were each given muster stations as we pulled into the driveway. Liam to help Richie prep the motorhome, Clara to get the pillows off the beds, Emma to get the sleeping bags, I was to pack perishable food from the refrigerator. Their mom had packed a huge box of crackers, cheese, fruit and bread for us which was safely stowed in the back of the car. Arriving home and true to our missions, each performed their tasks with efficiency and speed, as mechanics at a grand prix. Each person assumed their appropriate position, dutifully accomplished their task, then all jumped in and quickly the illustrious home on wheels, swung out onto the road right on time.

Spirits were high as we rolled up to the park gate, yes a site is available, success and we smiled happily as we navigated the narrow path to the site. There, I must admit, our smiles faded just a tad. It was a flat grassless site, jammed between two others and on looking around, we noticed we were actually surrounded by tents and campers; it was a sub-division in the woods, except a lot of trees seemed to be missing. Undaunted and determined not to let this minor problem spoil the weekend, Richie backed us into the site and out we got. Immediately the dogs on either side, tethered to long ropes began frantic barking and Sparky, not to be intimidated, rushed over to assert her authority. This quickly became a dog shouting match and three grandchildren tried in vain to suppress it. It was decided that while we set up things, perhaps Clara and Emma could take a walk to the beach and take Sparky with them. Meanwhile Richie, Liam and I would set up the picnic table, put out chairs and door mat and in no time it really was like home. We decided also that if we opened the large canopy, it would be a lovely shelter to sit under that evening and all next day.

Now we have never, in our past, owned a motorhome, therefore the intricacies of canopies opening and closing was not an operation we were familiar with. Richie commenced to pull at the metal poles on either side. They were quite reluctant to move, so he tried lifting one up. It came away quite easily, but it did not seem to fit anywhere, it wanted to lean and Richie wanted it to stand straight. Next he brought out his hammer, the sound of metal banging on metal brought me swiftly outside and away from my task of making up bunks. "Don't do that" I yelled, "surely that must be the wrong way if you have to use a hammer, why don't you ask the people over there how their canopy works?" I sensed Liam trying to distance himself from our camp site as he looked in the direction of the beach and his sisters. A fellow camper came over and he and Richie pondered, pushed, rattled and hit at the canopy, nothing moved. The camper left shaking his head, Richie took up the hammer again and it sprung open, wide open, on one side only. Now the problem was becoming serious, the metal frame seemed under stress, I warned Richie that he was looking at a major repair bill for the canopy, the children came back, the dogs started barking and Richie started swearing, loudly. Clara wandered off to make a fire for marshmallows, while Emma and Liam stood by with vacant looks. By now it was 7.30p.m., kids were hungry, tempers raw, dogs barking and Richie stuck under a sloping canopy threatening to kill the dog if he didn't shut up. I decided it's time out. Make some nice hot chocolate, make a nice big supper, forget the canopy for a while and enjoy what was left of the evening. As I went inside to put together a meal, I had a sickening thought. Going back to the doorway, I addressed my little group, "Who was to bring the box of groceries from the car?" Silence was the deafening reply, Clara looked at Liam, Liam looked at Emma, Richie looked at me, I looked at Richie. "Wonderful," I groaned, "no food" we had left the box of food in the car, hidden from sight under the false trunk floor. I looked at the half opened canopy, at Richie with his hammer and realized, driving to a restaurant was totally out of the question. Emma slunk away with her new cell phone to quietly send a text message: "Dad, it's a disaster."

But the camping Gods were not quite finished with us, the fire Clara had made had now burnt out, we had no more firewood, toasting marshmallow was now off the menu. Somehow, the whole thing became so utterly ridiculous, I just had to laugh, then Clara laughed, then Emma, then Liam even Richie cracked a grin. "We have eggs" I said, "lots of eggs."

Some good Samaritans appeared and within minutes the canopy was expertly erected, Richie was taught the simple procedure and we celebrated the success. Eating plates of fried eggs and fried up potatoes, we sat around the little table and re-lived the nightmare, laughing and pointing fingers until tears ran and as darkness came, we climbed wearily into warm cosy sleeping bags, "Tell us a story Richie" laughed the girls and with that and a promise that first thing in the morning we would pull up the steps and go home, we fell into a sleepy haze, listening to Richie's trailing voice, "When I was in Nova Scotia.........................."

But the devils work was not yet done, for as Liam snuggled down into his down bag, a plaintive voice whispered:-

"Grandma, Sparky pee'd on my sleeping bag."

And with that, we were all convulsed again everyone hooting and wide awake,

WORKING LIFE

ILLUSTRIOUS BEGINNINGS

My very first introduction to the working life came at the age of thirteen years. My best friend at school then was Brenda; we were inseparable, so much so that everyone at school referred to us as the "twinnies." Even the school theatre production that sought two close friends to play the brothers in the garden of Gethsemane instantly cast us. Between the afternoon and evening matinee shows, dressed as Arabs in long flowing robes and with coarse black beards stuck to our faces, we found eating sandwiches messy and hilarious.

But, I digress; in the summer of 1954, Brenda and I applied for and got the job of dishwashers at a small café in the Cleethorpes market place. Cleethorpes is the twin town of Grimsby and one town melts seamlessly into the other. In order to get there and add to the adventure, we decided we would take the train each day. Taking the short sixpenny ride, we would pretend that we were really going to work in London. The tracks ran along the coast as we entered the seaside town and since Cleethorpes was the end of the line we felt safe in the knowledge of ever really going very far at all. Just a short walk from the station was the market place, a large circular plaza surrounded by large terraced house, shops and a hotel. Two double decker buses had regular turn around here, one that went out to Humberston and the other into Grimsby. The plaza has one very narrow street leading into it from the main St. Peters Avenue, (also called "Heavens Gates" by bellowing bus conductors) this little street was so narrow that the bus filled the street and if you sat on the top deck of the bus and could open the windows, you would be able to almost touch the tops of the buildings on either side. The little café occupied a corner of this street and looked out onto the circular plaza. At the far end, another narrow road leads straight down to the promenade and beach. The sea, clearly visible and just a breath away casts up persistent fresh salty breezes. The café at that time catered mainly to holiday makers, since Cleethorpes was a popular seaside resort.

Our job was to wash and dry all dishes daily. There were no dishwashers, everything was done by hand and when we weren't busy with dishes, we had to make potato chips with a small chipper. Buckets of water containing fresh peeled potatoes were brought in and we dutifully punched them into perfect chips, taking the finished products into the adjoining kitchen to be fried. Occasionally the owner would bring us fresh raw liver that he had bought for his two Great Dane dogs. This we had to wash before he fed them to his dogs. As soon as the owner left, playing catch with the liver was an irresistible urge. The kitchen was quite large and for most of the day Brenda and I were alone. It was possible therefore to play catch until we got bored with it and we always ended up falling about in hysterical giggles as the slimy pieces of liver proved impossible to catch, sliding right out of our hands onto the floor. We would see how far across the kitchen we could throw to each other and standing one at each end of the kitchen wall we perfected our technique to the full distance.

Sometimes dishes were broken and not always by us. Several women worked in the adjacent kitchen too. The owner of the café came several times a week and sat up in his tiny attic office like Scrooge from the Dickens novel. One day he came thundering down the wooden stairs and announced to us all that too many dishes were broken and henceforth, employees would have to pay for every broken piece. The charge was established on a piece by piece item. Saucers and cups were three pence each and plates were sixpence. We thought that a great joke and I remember marching into the kitchen one day with a tray of freshly washed dishes announcing proudly "I have Thirty shillings and nine pence on this tray."

We were big fans then of Audrey Hepburn and joined her fan club. During lunch break, Brenda and I loved to browse Humphrey's department store on the High street. There we bought tan coloured neckerchiefs to wear with a crisp white blouse and tiered skirt from Marks and Spencer. To complement the chic Hepburn look, we also bought tan flat shoes with white socks. This was reminiscent of the outfit Audrey Hepburn wore in the movie *Roman Holiday.*

The money I earned that summer was to pay for a trip to Scotland with Brenda and her parents, however, that trip never matured, so I spent the money on a new bike. A Raleigh three speed with straight handle bars, in Kingfisher Blue. It would take me on many a great bike ride and get me to and from work when I became a full time employee at the age of fifteen years.

The following year saw me working on the Freeman Street market. This was a big outdoor market, in fact the only one in Grimsby at that time. The market had hundreds of stalls selling clothes, shoes, socks, meat, vegetables, drapes, toys, in fact just about everything. I worked for a tall stately and very kind elderly lady who had three prominent stalls at the front of the market. She always wore large hoop earrings and wore her flame red hair in a becoming chignon giving her the air of a vivacious gypsy. The first stall and closest to the street sold expensive nylons, 15 denier in black or beige, all with fancy seams running up the back. The nylon stocking were the sheerest you could buy and were like fine gossamer. Next to this, her second stall sold a variety of sweaters and tops. Her sweater stall was very popular and on a Saturday afternoon, women would be shoulder to shoulder along the front of the stall, pulling and pushing to get close and pick out a sweater. The sale of sweaters was always high. The third stall was my stall. I sold children's socks and shilling working stockings, otherwise known as lisle. These were thick stockings, always beige and 30 and 45 denier. Across from me was a man who occasionally also sold working stockings, sometimes he yelled out his ware, then I often countered back, in my best market voice, yelling "Shilling working stockings, children's socks!" At which he would scowl at me and hold a short truce then he would call out his wares again. I worked on the market for a full year, earning ten shillings a day every Saturday and sometimes on a Tuesday if there was no school. On cold rainy days or in winter, it was bitterly cold but my kindly employer always bought me a piping hot dinner. In the middle of the market was a small wooden building, more like a shed than anything else. At the front was an open counter where people could order take out fish and chips. If you would like to get into the long queue, you could go into the café at the back and sit on a cold chrome chair at a bare wooden table covered in oil cloth to eat meat pie and chips; or fish and chips, green mushy peas, a slice of bread and butter and a big white mug of tea. To say the "Pea Bung" was popular would be a gross understatement. Established in 1883 The Pea Bung was and still is one of the oldest chippys in town. You can enjoy freshly deep fried Grimsby fish with chips made from Lincolnshire potatoes and mushy peas on the side or you can take-away and enjoy. There was always a long line-up for the food, whether take out or eat in. My meal of meat pie, chips and mushy peas with gravy was always delivered from the Pea Bung at noon on a big white plate with a deep steel lid on the top to keep it hot. I devoured this hungrily at the stall in between selling my socks and stockings. It was always delicious and I loved it. If it was really cold, there was a portable paraffin heater placed just behind the stalls. I could stand over it to warm my hands when my fingers froze. My new best friend, Roy, always came at the end of the day to pick me up and ride home on the bus with me. What he was always too polite to tell me was that I had big black sooty rings round my eyes and nose from standing over that paraffin heater. When I got home and looked in the mirror I was mortified, staring back at me was a ghastly looking clown.

Next to our stalls was another lady, who reminded me of a gypsy too, short and stocky, with dark hair pulled back into a broad black net, she also wore the same gold loop earrings. Drapes and curtain remnants were for sale on her two stalls. One day I was given a piece of paisley fabric and I took it to a dressmaker. Betty made me a lovely sleeveless blouse with a mandarin collar which suited the fabric perfectly. When I showed the finished article to the gypsy lady she was so impressed she gave me another piece. This time it was cotton voile, white with small pink pin dots. This Betty made into another sleeveless blouse with miniature pearl buttons and a Peter Pan collar. Again, Betty knew instantly how to best use the fabric. Next I received a large piece of tartan taffeta and this was made into a three tiered skirt with a large cummerbund waist. One of the most stunning skirts I ever owned. I enjoyed working on the market; both of these ladies treated me always very kindly.

But at age fifteen, it was time to be working full time. I had wanted to stay at school one more year, in which I could learn typing and shorthand, but in my father's words, "Educating a woman is a waste of time." He was old school and said a woman's place was in the home. "She should be standing at the door with a clean frock on when the husband comes home" he declared. In that last year at school, a representative from the local employment office came to visit. Each girl was summoned to the office for a joint interview with the employment officer and headmistress. "Now what would you like to do when you leave school dear" I remember our headmistress saying to me benevolently. "Well", I ventured, "I kinda thought I would like to teach music in an infant school." At first the reaction was a stunning silence and then a ripple of laughter came from both women. "Oh no my dear," Miss Baker smiled, "You are an 'A' girl, 'A' girls go into offices, 'B' girls go into shops and 'C' girls go into factories." I was somewhat confused by this answer, but took it quietly as it seemed I had somehow not known about this rule. (I should explain here that the ABC remark was the system of slip streaming pupils. We were assessed on our school work, the brighter ones were classified as A, not so bright were in the B classes and the poor achievers were downed to C classes.) When we moved from Humberston to Grimsby, the headmistress assumed Cleethorpes education was not up to Grimsby standards and stated I should be placed in a "B" class. I was mortified by this and protested loud and strong, so much so that I was eventually allowed to start in 'A' with a warning I could be downgraded. Thankfully I never was, but if I had not fought, I am quite sure I would not have ever moved up. There was always that unstated feeling that B and C girls were in some way inferior to 'A' girls and I was not going down that road.

So being the good 'A' girl I was, I applied for an office job and started work soon after at a timber merchants on King Edward Street. I look back on my first real job interview with a wry smile. I was totally naïve, still at school and did not have much of a wardrobe fit for an interview. My school uniform of grey skirt, white blouse, blue tie, socks and brown shoes was pretty much it. The coat for school was a navy blue gabardine with a rain hood. So this was it then, but in an attempt to be more business - like I decided to forego the shoes and socks and wear my mother's red Cuban heel shoes with a pair of nylons bought from the market stall. I had never really worn a garter belt before: it was ridiculously uncomfortable and the seams on my nylons kept working round my legs so that they were twisted and insisted on snaking up the inside of my leg. The shoes also were a size too big so I stuffed the toes with newspaper. To add to the tragedy, it was pouring rain. When I arrived at the office, I sat across from the Manager, Mr. Arnold, who asked me a host of questions, then at the last decided to introduce me to the owner, Mr. Jack. He was the most polished and dauntingly professional looking man I had ever been introduced to, with his tweed suit, shiny brogues, short wavy blond hair and a meerschaum pipe sticking out of the side of his mouth; he reminded me of the famous pilot Douglas Bader. As his eyes cast over my bedraggled appearance and landed on my feet I felt an overwhelming pang of mediocrity, what a mess I must look. Riding to the interview on my bike in the rain, my legs were splashed with mud, the seams of my stockings had decided to settle for good and snaked lazily up the inside of my legs, the shoes obviously didn't belong to my feet and my face was splattered with rain. I left thoroughly dejected, quite sure I would not get the job. For reasons ever obscured to me, get it I did, maybe it was out of pity, but whatever, I enjoyed a very successful start as a working girl.

My job there was officially stated as "purchasing ledger clerk." This meant I had to enter all the day to day purchases in a big leather ledger, with pen and ink no less, no ball point pen. Apart from myself and Mr. Arnold, there was a secretary. Miss Pattinson and I were seated at a long desk which ran the full length of the office, under windows that faced onto King Edward Street. Mr. Arnold occupied a single desk in the middle of the room and on the far wall was a counter for making tea and coffee. Beyond that was the door to the private office of Mr. Jack Senior and Mr. Jack Junior. It was much like a Dickens office, but not cold and austere, nor were the owners mean. Quite the opposite and as time went by and I earned some money I could buy some clothes and new shoes. I gained confidence and enjoyed my job immensely. Miss. Pattinson was a great person to work with, she dressed very professional, wore impeccable makeup, her stocking seams were always straight and she helped me lots and loved to tease me, calling me, very affectionately, I might add "Ding Dong." There was a salesman who occasionally came in and I bristled as he gusted in, clapping his hands and declaring, "Tea, Miss. Thompson please", at which I had to sail to the back counter and make him his tea. Starting work in those days, you always were the junior, therefore the maker of tea, or occasionally coffee. The company paid for me to attend the College of Further Education one day a week, where I took English, Math, Bookkeeping and Commerce. This is where my entry into bookkeeping and eventually accounting has its roots, for I also went to night school three nights a week for Math, English and Fundamentals of Accounting, I enjoyed the assignments and bookkeeping especially.

I was very happy at the office, but after one year I had to give notice, as my father had decided to move to Canada. I told my friend Jane that I was leaving and that there would be a vacancy at the office, she promptly applied and got the job. Jane was from a more affluent family and did not have to battle wardrobe issues. She rode a motor scooter and was one of my closest friends. She was effervescent, brainy and very classy and jolly. We spent my final weeks there giggling and slipping notes to each other along the long desk as I relayed the vague intrigues of purchase journals. I have kept her little notes that she passed to me laughingly accusing me of leaving her all alone in the world.

Emma Peel

One of the most fascinating jobs I had was that of telephone sterilizer. In England, many businesses subscribed to a service in which the telephones would be cleaned and sterilized every week by an outside service. It was taken very seriously and carried out in a very professional manner.

Because my children were in school and would be home in the early afternoon, I found it much more convenient to find part time work so that I could be available to them when needed. The telephone sterilizing fit perfectly, as it required I work alone and as long as I made the round, I could manage my own time.

To start with, I had to go for training in Leeds. I took a train to the head Phonotas office and spent the day there learning how to professionally clean a handset, to polish the telephone, arrange the squares of cleaning paper neatly in my brief case and to properly sanitize the ear and mouth piece, also how to keep the phone active while doing all of the above. All equipment for the job was in a neatly fitted briefcase, the sterile solutions, the polish, the small rubber dumbbell that held the phone hooks down and lastly, the special squares of paper that are used for cleaning. These squares were meticulously held in the lid of the brief case and I was taught the special knack of fanning them so that they not only looked exceedingly organized, but were easy to retrieve. There was also a small pouch to put used squares into. Next I received a folding clip board, which held four sheets of various company names and the number of telephones on the premises. These were to be my customers, each in a different section of the town. To get to them all I would borrow my father's Morris Minor. I wore a purple suit that had a fitted jacket top, an A-line mini-skirt and high black stretchy go-go- boots. My briefcase was black with hard sides. When all put together, I decided I looked like Emma Peel of the Avengers, although Emma would never be caught driving the lowly Morris Minor.

My first day out with the local supervisor was very entertaining. The first days round was on an industrial estate called Pyewipe. We went into huge chemical factories, welding supply companies, fish curing plants and a construction site; going from office to office and cleaning every telephone as we went. The route usually ended at the reception desk, where we obtained a signature to validate our mission. The last call at the construction office turned out to be more than we bargained for. The sheet indicated that the single telephone was located in a trailer at the back of a large field and this was a new customer. For this reason, my supervisor went to check exactly where it was and told me to stay in the car. After what seemed only minutes, I saw her running from the long grass to the car in obvious panic. Panting and gasping for breath, she jumped in the car.
"What's the matter?" I asked.
"Ruddy great horse" she said breathless.
Apparently there was a large Alsatian guard job and it had come bounding through the long grass straight at her, at which she turned and ran. She had no intention of going "back there" she said, so that ended my first day. I delivered the car back to the docks and caught the bus home feeling charged with excitement.

So now I am on my own and it feels liberating and adventurous. I first take a bus down to the dockyards and I walk along the large wharves. It's bustling with lumpers (stevedores) unloading trawlers, row upon row of cases of freshly caught fish, women in white overalls wearing large wooden clogs and men in thick yellow oilskin aprons filleting the days catch. A wolf whistle rings clear through the cacophony of a busy fish dock and the women eye me with suspicion. I am an alien threat here with my briefcase and go-go boots, I am not one of them and the women make sure I know it. My dad has heard the whistles too and comes out of the machine shop to silently hand me the car keys and I thankfully get behind the wheel to hit the road again. It didn't take long to familiarize myself with the different routes and companies and every day was a new adventure. There were large corporations such as British Oxygen, who would later offer me a job as a saleswoman selling welding supplies; a small radio station that let me see all the controls for broadcasting and ship to shore communication, a funeral parlour that was the front room of a home owned by a sweet old lady, warehouses, a frozen food factory and the list went on.

Some of the companies hold special memories for me, such as the funeral parlour. It was the end house of a long row of terraced homes, typical of the many row houses in town and the same as the ones both of my grandmothers lived in. Mrs. Mac had rented her front room to a small funeral director. It was the ordinary front living room, small and square with a single sash window that looked on to the street. The door between this room and the rest of the house was locked. I had therefore to first go to the back garden and shout over the top of a high brick wall "Mrs. Mac, Mrs. Mac!" This was the signal for Mrs. Mac to unlock the parlour door and let me in through the front of the house. There was one telephone on a side bureau and a wooden chair on each side of the fireplace. Sometimes a solitary coffin sat on a dais in the middle of the room. Mrs. Mac would stand and chatter to me as I cleaned the phone and if I had time, I would go back into her little kitchen for a cup of tea. We had lovely little chats and I think she enjoyed it as much as I did. She sent me letters after I moved to Canada and signed off always with "you was a lovely lass."

The security guard office at the big frozen food factory always had a cup to tea waiting for me when I came back from making the factory round, which was large with over fifty telephones. I went to countless fish houses on the docks; one had a hungry rabid guard dog tied to a chain. The chain came only inches from a wooden ladder I had to climb to get up to a bombed out office on the top floor. The building had been bombed in the war and part of the ceiling had a gaping hole in it and was never repaired. In a makeshift office sat a dirty old couch, a coffee table and a telephone hung on the wall so full of fish scales you couldn't see the original black Bakelite. The dog downstairs at the ladder, going savage and yanking at his chain, waited with no small amount of patience for me to descend again. I thought it a fabulous salesman indeed to convince these people they needed to clean their telephone.

There were several dogs along the way, including the one in the long grasses that went out to greet my supervisor at the construction site. As I made my way there the following week, alone through the long grass, I crept slowly and carefully towards the trailer. I made it, heart thumping like a deer in flight, to the side door of the trailer. All was quiet and no sign yet of the animal, so quietly and stealthily I tip-toed through to the living quarters at the front of the trailer. At the same time, a man came creeping up from the opposite direction. We came face to face in the narrow hall and startled each other.
"What are you doing?" he demanded.
"I'm here to clean the phones" I replied. "I'm scared of the dog."
"What" he laughed, "You're afraid of Rinty?"
Then he did something that saw my whole life pass before me.
"KILL" he commanded, turning to Rinty, at his side and pointing to me at the same time.
I could feel my knees turn to jelly and stood frozen to the floor, bracing myself for the lunge. But instead, Rinty looked confusedly to me then the owner, clearly puzzled and not understanding at all what he was supposed to do. Flopping down on all fours, he rolled over, gave a short sigh and went back to sleep. Both the man and I looked at each other and burst out laughing.
"He won't hurt ya."
Well, thanks a lot, good to know I thought and relieved to be able to breathe again. From then on the trek through the long grass

was always a cautionary ramble. Sometimes Rinty would come bounding to me; sometimes he would be silently spying down on me from some grassy knoll, other times he just lay on the floor of the trailer, watching me through lazy eyes as I cleaned the phone. I seldom saw the construction foreman again, it was just Rinty and me and we developed a 'nice to see ya' kind of bond.

Another guard dog was at the warehouse of a great fruit storage plant. This was a large wooden building, in the shape of a *U*, with the straight lines being long loading bays. Doors along the bay led into the sides of the warehouse. One door however, a wooden door with faded and peeling green paint, was always closed and had one tiny barred window at the top. It had the look of a prison door. The first time I approached this warehouse, I eyed the shabby exterior from the car with apprehension. It looked forbidding and I felt uneasy about going inside. My sheet said there were two telephones in the office and as yet I had no idea where that might be in this seemingly last outpost of civilization. My feelings were not eased as I walked up the ramp to the loading bay. I would have to walk the full length of the bay to the main building. A couple of luckless looking men came out and stood in a menacing pose at the end of the ramp. I put on my best business air, tried to stand as tall as my five foot frame would allow and proceeded to march deliberately up the ramp. Suddenly from the prison door, this huge snarling savage dog lunged at me through the tiny window. I jumped so hard that I almost fell off the ramp. The men at the far end sneered amongst themselves and I felt like the prim and proper idiot they obviously had cast me as.

The office was easier to find than I imagined and was just inside the big warehouse door. Inside, my sheltered existence got another smack and I was not prepared for the site before me. It was a large, overcrowded and messy office, the air dense and smelling of cigars. In the middle of this small garrison, sat two large wooden desks, pushed together to face each other.

Facing each other also, identical male twins and the most obese people I had ever seen. Above them on one wall, a large picture of a pair of trousers, presumably belonging to one of men I saw before me, with two men standing inside one of the pant legs. These were the "The Brothers." The desks were a mess of papers and firmly planted in the middle, a big open bottle of whisky. The brothers surveyed me coolly, leaning back on their huge chairs; they slowly puffed on big round cigars. Warily I pushed a few papers to the side on a desk and opened my briefcase. Then in as formally and professional a manner I could muster dutifully cleaned each telephone. Silence had descended in the air, a couple of the men from the loading bay had slouched in and stood hand in pockets watching the show. Tweedledum and Tweedledee sat in icy silence and watched my every move. Finally done, I silently passed my log sheet to be signed. One of the brothers signed, I packed up my briefcase and swung it down by my side, marched deliberately out, feeling the heat of stares on my back and praying I wouldn't slip as I went back down the loading bay. As I got half way down, I heard a voice shout "Give her an orange" and looking back, I saw one of the brothers leaning against the office door. A smirking boor dashed into a side door and came out with a huge Jaffa orange and plonked it into my hand. I didn't allow my disbelief to show until I was safely sitting in the car and then grinning like the cat that got the cream wryly looked back on the premises. I felt like Joan of Arc, having just conducted a raid into an enemy encampment and had now arrived home without a scratch. Ah! the sweet taste of victory over adversity. The brothers and their warehouse became one of my most favourite clients. The following week, everything happened exactly as before, but this time the cry from the office was "Give her an apple and an orange!" and after only a few weeks I would be leaving with a plastic grocery bag full to the brim with every variety of fresh fruit. The brothers and I never exchanged a word, but we had a silent respect for each other and I loved going there ever after. In fact, walking down the street, briefcase in one hand and bag of fruit in the other, I was greeted by a friend with a huge smile on his face and exclaiming "You've been to "The Brothers" again haven't you." "Yep" I grinned.

I look back on that job with nostalgia. The amount of friendly people I met, the interesting occupations that I witnessed, the freedom of being alone, provided a perfect mix and at the same time, paying me for doing it. I have a special place in my heart for Rinty and I rarely reach for an orange without I see "The Brothers", sitting in their smoky office, big cigars hanging from stern lips and sipping whisky from a bottle.

OFFICE DAZE

Since lately when I get home from work I seem not to have the time or energy to write my journal I have decided to write a few pages at work. Work has been a source of boredom lately, so much so that I think I can do this job blindfold. I really should be looking for something more meaningful, but I plan to retire soon, so in the meantime, I suffer. Personalities are getting to me and this, the second week of March, seems to have brought out a dose of cabin fever in all inmates. For instance, Mona right now is driving me "nuts" with 'He who must be obeyed' a close second. Both Amanda and I are commiserating with each other and Amanda says she has told Jessica flat, that she will not take any more of Carl's "attitude" lying down. She said also that if Carl treats her with disrespect she will treat him likewise (way to go Amanda). I think both Mona and Carl are cast from the same die; both seem to think they are of the "race that knows Joseph." And if I hear once more how "wonderful" Carl's son is and how so unique in every way; or how unfortunate Mona's life has been, since her famous "third organ damage" which she unfortunately received at the hands of some incompetent surgeon, or that her sister is allowed more time off without penalty, I shall positively barf. Carl, on the other hand, also seems to think we lesser mortals have no idea of good taste, we do not know in fact what life is all about and we certainly could never presume to know the joy of, say, a good restaurant, or even how to save a homeless person, as he has just spent the last hour telling us. (He took the man a cup of soup). Right now, I have the strongest urge to go out into the main office and shout "OK everybody-stop work for a second and come out here-let me tell you of a little incident – or let me show you some pictures of my holiday (and here a little chuckle). Out we trundle, Lord have mercy on us.

Mona has not (these are Amanda's words) worked a full week since last July and she is still whining and complaining she is under too much stress because: a) her mother died last year, b) because she fell rollerblading and got a concussion (this by the way is the perfect excuse for making any mistakes at work) and c) still suffering from the afore mentioned third organ damage. Guess I am in a sour mood, for I could go on for ages.

Blade came over last Sunday, another blunder on my part. He bought a bottle of Jackson Triggs, my favourite and says he wants us to go cycling in Europe. That would be lovely and right up my street, but Oh, its Blade, really not the right fit, he seems somewhat slow and it bothers me. For instance, he turned up in that damned black silk overcoat, which has a huge rip up the back almost to the shoulder. I noticed it last time we went to the ballet (he wore it over a tuxedo, for the afternoon matinee for heaven's sake) he looked positively stupid and I was mortified. This is the karma of my life just now.

The weather on the other hand is bright and sunny, cold but plus three degrees. Snow is forecast for tonight, about 15cm. Spring is just around the corner and I can't wait to get in the garden. Will have to put a new roof on this year and would like to finish one bedroom and the living room, pretty tall order on the money I make. It's all pay out and so very tiring.

Am reading Land of Shadows on the train, it's about Grey Owl and I find he had a much more interesting life than I did.

Penny Buns

At the age of seventeen my father quit Canada and I found myself back in England, working now at a large fish meal company. The plant had five factories which manufactured animal feed from fish offal. The office block was at the end of the line of factories and consisted of two floors. It was a modern red brick building with rows of Georgian style windows. You entered up a small semi-circular staircase through large double front doors. On the top floor was the typist pool, the boardroom and the executive offices. On the ground floor was the accounting office, cashier office, drafting office and janitors room. I started in the cashier office. We were a team of four, seated in a row by the front windows. Mr. Brumby was the head cashier, a wiry intense version of Friar Tuck with his bald head and wispy circle of faded brown hair. He had small beady eyes, a sallow complexion and always wore a black suit, so old it shone. In front of him sat Mr. Darlington. Again, in his early sixties, he had thinning dark grey hair, a decidedly ruddy complexion, large eyes and bulbous nose. He always wore the same tweed jacket, which he seemed to have outgrown, as it didn't meet at the front and the sleeves were too short. He always wore the same grey pants and a sweater over his shirt, all tucked neatly underneath the tweed. I sat in front of Mr. Darlington. Across the room sat Mr. Kyle. He was quite young and handsome, with blue eyes, blond wavy hair, but that was the extent of his youth. His mannerisms and dress matched the two old codgers, with the same tweed jacket (but his still fit his younger frame) the same sweater over shirt and grey pants. All of the men rode bikes to work, so all came in with bicycle clips on their pants which they took off at their desks.

At tea break, the three old codgers as I liked to call them would stop and gossip, just like a bunch of women. Either some current affair, or some beef about their job, all the while smoking cigarettes. Mr. Darlington went to great lengths to 'roll his own' and would pace up and down the office with his little tin of tobacco and his little roll of woodbine papers. I was never part of these dialogues; it was strictly a man session, so occasionally I went across to accounting which was all girls. We had our own little gossip session over tea and once I decided to rehearse the scene of a conversation just concluded with Mr. Darlinton, who was giving me some fatherly advice upon my recent engagement.

"So, Miss Thompson, you are going to be married." (Policy dictated we did not use first names at work)
"Yes, Mr. Darlington"
"Well", said Mr. Darlington, pacing the floor and rolling a thin cigarette, "Two cannot live as cheaply as one."
"No, Mr. Darlington"
"Because a penny bun, Miss Thompson, will now cost tuppence
"Yes, Mr. Darlington"

At which I simply had to leave the room for fear of laughing out loud and ran straight into the accounting office.
Next day, the head secretary told me she had been sitting on the bus on the way home after work last night when she started thinking about my little charade and had suddenly, in the middle of the bus, burst into an uncontrollable fit of laughing. I don't think Mr. Darlington ever knew how much mileage we got out of that priceless little bit of pre-nuptial advice.

I eventually applied for and got a transfer to accounting as a comptometer operator. I loved working on the comptometer. It's a super interesting machine to calculate on and the company quickly bought a new electric model that could turn over so fast, it purred.

Years later, I found myself back in Canada again. As a mom of two toddlers, I looked for evening work and found a job at the

CIBC clearing house downtown. I worked evenings, 6.00 p.m. to 11.30 p.m. so that I could be home all day with my two little tots and their Dad was home with them in the evenings.

It was more like factory work, as it was a huge floor, with rows and rows of wooden tables that were grouped into different teams. Each team consisted of about six women. We waited, not long, for trucks to come in and unload sacks of bundled cheques from the various bank branches. We would get several sacks at a time and these were emptied onto the tables and we sorted them using the MICR coding on the bottom of the cheque. Rows and rows of cheque bundles would cover each table. Once they were sorted, we loaded them into trays lined up on an angle on large mobile shelves and wheeled them to the data room. This was a room that was just as big as the room we worked in. It was permanently closed off and had rows and rows of huge IBM 1540 reader/sorters. After a few months of working there I was offered training on the sorters. This was a good step-up and working the machines was totally fascinating. The sorters could sort 60,000 cheques an hour and it involved you wheeling the large mobile shelves to the side of a sorter and feeding bundles of cheques into its hungry yaw. The machine was large, standing about 6 ft. tall and 10 ft. long. It had a pressure arm at the front and to one side where cheques were loaded. As they were sorted, they fell into one of 13 pockets, also pressure armed. The pressure arms sounded like air brakes. The goal was to keep the machine running and not stop. If the feed arm emptied, the machine stopped, at the same time, if any pocket filled to more than about six inches the machine stopped again. This kept you fantastically busy, grabbing a handful of cheques from the shelf, filling the feed arm and keeping pockets from over filling and then spinning round to put sorted pockets on a new mobile shelf unit. And since cheques were whipping through at about 1000 per minute, it was a challenge; time flew when you were on the sorter. Other things could stop the machine also, a staple in a cheque or someone writing a cheque and eating a jam sandwich at the same time and you'd be surprised how many people do that.

I loved working the sorter and had my name posted on the notice board, the fastest time on a sorter by a beginner, over 57000 cheques on my first attempt. It was a crazy machine and I loved it. A few months later I was offered a promotion to supervisor, but we were on the move again, this time back to England and I had to refuse.

COMMUTER WARS

Wednesday, March 29th, 2000

Just another uneventful day-this boring routine is slowly killing me. Everyday it's dash to the GO stations, cancel my ticket at the machine, run down a flight of steps only to run up another flight to Platform 3, then walk the full length of the platform (in the brutal weather for its outdoors) just so that I can get a seat on the last carriage. I stand and watch the red-wing blackbirds as they flit among scrub and low bushes beside the tracks, heralding the first signs of spring. They caw and screech noisily and the bright red of their wing is vivid amongst the dull tall grasses. A man comes every morning with three cups of coffee for his friends who are already on the platform; we are almost to a nodding acquaintance. An obnoxious elderly couple always appears and they try to push in to the front as we board, he fairly tramples over me. They cunningly station themselves apart so they can "cover" both doors. Once on, they go straight for the back seat (my seat) I always sat there before they muscled in on the scene. Furthermore, if the woman gets there first, she stands guard over the seat, blocking the aisle and waits for "he." Such strange and territorial people in this world, I just stand back and watch their anxiety play out in them.
One day however, the Gods smiled on me, I got there first and swiped their seat! They sat across the aisle clearly rattled, feathers ruffled all the way to the big smoke and I sat like the proverbial cat that got the cream and smiling quietly, did my crossword

A Grey Nomad

Into the Unknown

Driving to the airport on a cold and icy New Year's Eve, we watched in mutual silence as the gloomy scene passed by our car window. With a lump in my throat and a sinking feeling in my stomach, I felt as if I had a date with a surgeon. What had I been thinking? Overwhelming feelings of guilt at "abandoning" my family alternated with fears of traveling alone left me on the verge of tears. I had never travelled alone, but in my usual impulsive way I had signed on to a one week sailing course in the British Virgin Islands. Now a thousand worries blurred my mind. There was a connection in Puerto Rico, what if I miss it? I can't even speak that language! What if I mess up while sailing, how will I cope living on a yacht for seven days with complete strangers? As we walked to the gate I turned to say goodbye and prayed my husband would say "Don't go, let's do this together someday." At the departure gate I searched his face for a sign, but his steady gaze and impassive look told me nothing. Muttering a soft goodbye I turned doggedly round and walked towards the customs officer.

"Where are you going?"

"British Virgin Islands" I whispered and with trembling hands I pushed my passport at him.

"Where?" he demanded

As if ashamed of the very word, I looked about me and repeated softly "The British Virgin Islands." He looked at me over the desk and frowned. Now another officer joined him.

"What are you going to do there?"

"Sail" I gulped.

My heart began to beat a jagged rhythm and a lump floated up to my throat. Why won't he let me through? Why is he so suspicious? I felt doomed I wanted to go home.

"How much money do you have?" asked the second officer.

"A hundred dollars"

"Is that all?" he said incredulously.

"Isn't that enough?" I cried and mentally made a quick review of the course outline. The brochure had said "*fully provisioned*" and "*only spending money required*" what else should I have brought?

Remembering our itinerary, I quickly thrust the crumpled paper on his desk. Reading it carefully he eyed me with a cool official stare before silently nodding me on my way.

With no small relief I dragged my bags and sagging confidence to the boarding gate.

On the long flight I sat glued to my seat. Feeling like an escapee and hiding inside the pages of a book I took a deep breath and tried to relax.

Sailing was not new to me; I started sailing lessons in England, in that basic of boats a "Mirror" and on a cold grey reservoir at that. More recently, for one evening a week I self-indulgently dropped the shackles of wifely and motherly duties and crewed on a small sail boat, this time upping the ante on a "Shark." But a little knowledge is a dangerous thing. I found the freedom intoxicating. Mothering and playing the domesticated woman had been my all, but in recent years an unsettling wind was blowing across the flat and endless prairie that seemed to be shaping into my life.

Arriving at Puerto Rico I found young people milling around in several groups. They had various types of kit bags piled around the floor. Peering at them over my book, I decided they looked like sailors and the stress level dropped a degree.

Suddenly standing beside me was a young girl, all tan and sandals and thick black hair.

"Who's boat are you on?" she asked.

"Scott.…. I think"

"Oh so am I, I'm Dina, what's your name?"

"Diane"

"Our group is over there" she said, pointing across the floor. "Come on over."

We were a crew of five, plus an instructor. I learned we were also the lead boat of a flotilla of eight boats. My confidence edged up a notch. These were great people; I liked every one of them and imagine that, I'm on the lead boat! I grew an inch!

After another short flight and a hair rising roller coaster motor boat ride across a sweep of deep blue ocean we arrived at the island of Tortola. There I boarded a sleek forty two foot yacht named *Susa Karibe* and felt immediately at home. After stowing our gear we all headed up to an open air restaurant. By now our group had swelled to forty eight and became one large extended family. After dinner there was dancing under the stars as everyone waited for the midnight hour. Fanned by a soft ocean breeze, the palm trees swayed and whispered and in the distance you could hear the faint throbbing of waves beating upon the shore. Standing at the edge of the dance floor I gazed out to sea and drank in the warm salty air. My senses were dazzled, intoxicated and as bongo drums began to pulse, I warily stepped out of the shadow, determined to dance into this New Year, even if I had to do it alone!

Hoisting sails, tacking up wind, or just laying at anchor, the crew of the *Susa Karibe* was a tanned, highly capable lean mean machine. Each night in our cabin we slept like babies, rocked by the waves, the sea sang us a lullaby.

My impetuousness has been cause for concern to some who think a "woman's place is in the home." But a woman marries, takes her husband's name, becomes "the wife" then "the mother" little nibbles at your soul. Like Persephone eating the pomegranate seed, I sometimes slip away into the other world. This sailing adventure was my latest slip. On my desk now is a picture that I often fondly look at, it is of five people. They are assembled around the mast of a large white yacht. In front is a slim thirty something woman who is looking directly into the camera. Tanned and windswept she looks happy and confident as she kneels on one knee, her chin cupped in her hand. Her mouth is twisted in a wry smile. She is me.

IN SEARCH OF GREY OWL

A constant reader, I happened on the works of Grey Owl and instantly became a devotee, reading all I could of him and by him. To me, he was a powerful story teller, passionate about the wilderness and champion of the First Nations People and a life-long advocate for the vanishing beaver. For a while, he lived with the Anishnabai Ojibwa of Bear Island and married there. It was easy steps therefore, that after an eight day canoe trip on Lady Evelyn Lake in Temagami, I would spend a weekend with the first nations on Bear Island, meet the descendants of Temagami Ned, stand on the spot where Grey Owl married Agnes and experience the spirit of the places he touched. This is my journal entry of that weekend.

June 30th, 2000

Gliding over smooth waters, we paddled back to Mowat Landing on this our last day. My canoe partner today was Howard and after stowing gear and loading canoes, we have all set a new destination..... the book store at Haileybury. An old and interesting store, it has a reputation for its rows and rows of books, both old and new. I bought a map of our trip and searched in vain for "O rugged land of Gold" by Martha Martin. Howard bought "Pilgrims of the Wild" since I garbled on so much about Grey Owl he has now caught the bug. Gord bought a book of "Knots" and one on the Sioux uprising, we have all suddenly become interested in all things native. Keith, our trip leader says I should have brought a Grey Owl book with me and read it to the group nightly! This was a highly successful trip and I have earned a free "Natural Outings" T-shirt which Pauline has promised to mail to me, Howard is going to send me information on the Bookbinders Guild, Gord says he hopes we meet again, Gertrude is going to call in September to go canoeing and as I walked back to my car, Keith called out "You are a good canoeist" Ah! BJ put that in your pipe and smoke it!

I hurried straight from the Access Road to meet Virginia; she is supposed to meet me at the wharf to go over to Bear Island and is late already. Virginia runs a small establishment on the Island teaching First Nation lore and customs. I will stay there for three days and two nights. After one hour and a half cooling my heels, an aluminum boat comes storming across the water and comes to a splashing halt at the wharf. Out climbed a dark skinned Indian girl whose long black hair hung thick and untidily over her shoulders. I walked over and asked if she was Virginia and - she was. We loaded my daypack, boots and sleeping bag into the front of the boat and set off under cloudy skies and over choppy waters. I was wrong to assume this would be a pleasant boat ride. Before you could say "Hàu" we were besieged by yet another aluminum boat, whose sole occupant it seemed was intent on running clear over us. Flashing a broad grin, long black hair flying wildly in the wind, the driver aimed his boat at us with such a mortifying speed I felt sure I was going down to Davey Jones locker instead of the peaceful land of Hiawatha. This was a resident from the island deciding to play "chicken" with us and while Virginia yelled "Hey, Hey, Hey" he aimed his boat directly at us veering away only at the last minute, then waving and grinning, he tore over to the landing. My heart beating like an Indian *War Drum, I felt I had just escaped a brush with death. Virginia calmly said "he always teases me."*

Virginia says she was not sure I was coming – meaning- she was ill prepared - we stop first at her house for supplies - food-water-towels etc. Standing at her open fridge door she offers me cheese buns, coffee, juice – anything that comes to mind. There is a friend visiting from Arizona; Janice is a Hopi Indian with striking features, small slanting eyes, high cheek bones, red/brown skin and again that lovely long black straight hair.

Her steady gaze and gentle nod tells me she is a very gentle and quiet sole.

At last we are off in the boat to the other side of the Island and there on a point is the most awesome sight. Two enormous Tipi's of white canvas, with large poles sticking out of the top, to each of which are tied coloured ribbons. I will learn later that each pole represents a value; Obedience, Kindness, Humility, Respect, Love, Faith, Strength, Cleanliness, Happiness and Hope. The crosshatches that hold the front flaps together represent relationship and two long poles coming from the back manoeuvre the fire flaps that can be turned to suit the wind direction. The Tipi's are set amongst the tall pines and one (mine) is close to the water's edge.

Stepping ashore, Virginia asks if I am comfortable sleeping alone or would I like to share the other Tipi with her, her husband and Janice. I assure her I am quite comfortable to go it alone and so she introduces me to my new quarters. I am surprised at the spaciousness inside, a fire ring is set at the centre and along three walls are sleeping bunks made of logs and branches. Two large logs serve as end tables and by the door flap is a pile of fresh cut logs. I put my nylon sleeping bag on a bunk and another is quickly piled on top by Virginia. Mine will catch the sparks she says hers will not. I am quite happy in my new house and already am looking forward to turning in for the night.

Next we went up to an octagonal building serving as a kitchen and where Virginia puts on a fresh pot of coffee. The building is new and has a propane stove and refrigerator. The lighting is all by oil lamp and Doug (her husband and band chief) has made a water system that is gravity fed from the lake. Everything is spotlessly clean and well equipped for guests. Pretty birch baskets hold red flowers and moose antlers hang from the ceiling. I am given a flashlight to take back to my Tipi.

Back down by the water's edge I laze on a chaise lounge sipping fresh coffee and soak in the peaceful vista which is Temagami. The water gently laps at the shore, the ribbons on the poles flutter in the breeze and inside my Tipi I see the glow of the fire, which Virginia has just built and will not die out for my entire stay. I sigh and feel I have been blessed by some unseen force which has brought me to this spot where it seems I was ever meant to be.

As supper time approaches, Janice, Virginia and I take to the boat once again for a mad dash across to the centre of the lake to a local restaurant called The Looney Bar. Virginia has bought for me and her, roast beef dinner with gravy, while Janice has a looney burger. Finding that I love chocolate, Virginia has bought me six mars bars!!!! Janice and I consume them that night.

On the wall of the Looney Bar is an awesome life size pencil drawing of Grey Owl by Don O'Sullivan. It is the famous study of Grey Owl with a beaver curled around his neck. What wouldn't I give to have that drawing? I sit and gaze at it and wish it could be mine, as here it sits in all its quiet simplicity. I wonder if other patrons are as drawn to it as I am, as they sit hungrily chewing on their hamburgers.

That evening I met Doug who came to the point to join us. Doug is very quiet, soft spoken, but a large burly man with short black wavy hair. Over the weekend we have long discussions about many subjects that I find of great interest; treaty rights, the Indian Temperament (Doug says they base all their decisions on emotion rather than thought) on Grey Owl and the people who knew him. He was very interesting to talk to, but at his core is very reserved and shy. Finally it came time to say goodnight, Virginia gave me a large Indian blanket to cover the door. We stoked up my fire with lots of wood so that inside my wigwam. was the cosiest place on earth. I climbed into my sleeping bag and gazed up through the vent flap, at the stars and the spirit ribbons wafting in the breeze. The sky dressed in dark blue, the fire crackling and hissing and I, I fell blissfully asleep to the sounds of a loons call, sure as God made little green apples that I had found Utopia.

But even in Paradise, work has to be done and in the early hours of the morning I awoke to find my fire was down to a glimmer of ashes. So tearing the birch bark strips as I had been shown and adding fresh kindling, it soon became a roaring blaze again, whereupon I once more sank into the peaceful sleep of the innocent. Then as the morning sun rose up, I heard my Ziploc bag rustling and saw a squirrel checking out my pack. There is a gap between the walls of the Tipi and the ground of about eight inches and he had no problem coming in.

Next morning, after climbing out of my sleeping bag I jumped into the lake to bathe and jumped out just as quick - it was freezing cold! But I did feel refreshed and had a chance at last to wash my hair after a week on Lady Evelyne. Then it was up to the kitchen to join our party, (Doug, Janice and Virginia) for breakfast of fresh pickerel and scrambled eggs, toast, juice and coffee. Next we got together a picnic basket and Doug drove Virginia and me over to a narrow inlet. We crept up among the logs and shallows so far up I was totally impressed with Doug's canoe handling. He perched the boat up on the water's edge and we climbed out into the bush to hike part of an old portage trail-complete with black flies and mosquitoes. Doug pointed out an abandoned canoe in the bush, he said it had been a cedar strip from the early 1900's, "probably Grey Owl's" he remarked dryly.

A lunch of tasty hamburgers on a fire hastily made by Doug and Virginia from surrounding brush was enjoyed lakeside, I took pictures, but Doug too shy to pose kept right on cooking and smiling.

The afternoon was spent lazing in my chaise lounge, reading and dozing. Evening saw us eating a huge dinner of BBQ Steak, beans, potato salad and rolls, followed by fresh strawberries and coffee. We sat around the fire ring just outside of the Tipi; the air was balmy with a warm gentle breeze off the lake. We all four sat by the fire, fireflies lit up the air and Virginia brought out her drum. She warmed up the skin by the fire and eventually picked it up to beat a slow steady rhythm and softly sang an old Indian love song, whaaaawhooooeeeeeyaaaaooooooeeeoh. And as I sat back and listened to those unfamiliar words; heard the soft beat of the drum; looked up to the tall pines standing around us, black against the night sky; watched the fireflies dance through the air; smelled the smoke from the fire and the scent of the pines; saw the Tipi glow against the fire within, I was transported to another time and another world. It was one of life's most magical moments and the earth seemed to be at peace with itself. Virginia sang louder and the drum beat continued its steady beat, the fire crackled and spit and the forest loomed in ponderous silence as we gazed transfixed into the flickering flames. The water gently lapped against the rocky shore and far out in the lake a loon called. "They are calling for wind" said Doug-"that is what the Anishnabai believe."
I asked Virginia, "What is that song?"
"It is a woman's song" she said, "It asks the spirits for help"
The wind sighed with me and I felt an overwhelming sense of peace.
After the songs, the drum was laid to rest, we popped corn and sat around the fire just talking and gazing into the fire until I felt sleepy and rising to go to my bed of logs and twigs, bid a soft goodnight to my hosts to sleep the sleep of the blissfully contented.

Next morning after a slow start we ate breakfast of bagels, ham, boiled eggs, honey, juice and coffee. I asked Virginia to scrub the hike to the watch tower and instead let's go to the library to see the Grey Owl pictures and see where he was married. She

*showed me lots of photographs, Temagami Ned, old trapper
pictures, pictures of past chiefs, all of them just sitting carelessly
in the draw of an old wooden desk. These are the very same
pictures that were part of the movie "Grey Owl" by Richard
Attenborough and starring Pierce Brosnan. On the library
wall a diagram of the Bear Island Family tree and there it was:
"Angel m Archie Belany." I stood on the very spot that Archie
and Angel had stood to get married.*

*Virginia had some business to attend to so I was dropped off
at the home of Hugh Mackenzie - an Ojibwa artist of some
renown – and a cousin of Doug. He has a small cottage next
door to Virginia and Doug and I was invited in to view some of
his art work. These are acrylic paintings, decidedly native in
style. His painted Canada Goose is used by Linda Lundstrom
on her silk scarves and the fine detailed drawings of the Blue
Jay are made famous by the Toronto Blue Jays in their gift shop.
I bought some note cards and a Blue-Jay T-shirt. But the best
was yet to come. Walking across the room, Hugh picked up his
electric guitar.*
"Ever heard of Chet Atkins?" he asked.
"Yes" I replied, wondering what was to come.
*He promptly turned on his computer, inserted a diskette of Chet
Atkins and dumbfounded me with the most amazing concert
of guitar playing. He played right along with the diskette,
never missing a note, a chord or vibrato. When he stopped
I was so disappointed and asked him to play some more. He
willingly obliged and played "In the mood" while I took his
picture. Completely self-taught and very modest, this man was
exceedingly talented.*
*"It's all practice" he said "Just you sit there and relax" and he
played to me once more.*
I finally had to leave when Virginia came back to pick me up.
"You can email me anytime" he called as I left his house.
My, can that man play a guitar.

Virginia then took me on a tour of the community hall and various offices before heading back to the mainland. We sped through the water again at speedboat pace and as quick as a wink I was back on the mainland and all was behind me.

So now I am back in Toronto, I do not hear my beloved white throat here yet he sang to me every day in Temagami. On Bear Island, if he was not above the Tipi, he was right next door and he greeted me every morning. Talking with Virginia about finding your personal totem, I believe I found it that weekend in the tiny white throated sparrow. As Virginia pointed out, "he does seem to attract you most of all."

It was my great privilege to spend a weekend on Bear Island with Doug, Virginia and Janice.
Their generous hospitality, the songs and lessons I learned of the Ojibwa life, the peace and tranquility of Bear Island, sleeping in my own Tipi and a chance to walk in the footsteps of Grey Owl are memories that will live in my heart for always.

The white throated sparrow, or spring sparrow, or Canada Bird:-

His plaintive unfinished melody can be heard everywhere in the North Woods during the summer months. He stands with the Beaver and the Pine Trees as a symbol of the wilderness.
And because to the Indian ear his song echoes the phrase "All is well, all is well" to have one of these birds sing in a tree under which a person is standing is considered an omen of future happiness.
The White Woodsman translates his song: O O O Can-a-da-Can-a-d-a Can-a-da While the Indian claims he sings Me-me-me-no-ta-kiy-no-ta-kiy-no-ta-ky-ah

WILDERNESS CAMPING: ATLIN, B.C.

Soon after my divorce, amongst the many challenges of adjustment was the question of vacations. I had virtually no experience travelling alone. A trip to the restaurant could be daunting, even with the single woman's constant companion, a book, in which to hide ones alone-ness. So when Peter, a colleague at work, hung up in the office a poster of a wilderness/ art camp in the remote community of Atlin in Northern British Columbia, I was double dared. The poster promised canoeing, hiking, wilderness camping plus various art classes, one of which was photography. I wanted desperately to go, but agonized for days. How could I possibly travel so far all alone?

"It's simple" chirped Peter, "You fly to Edmonton, take a bus to Jasper, the dome train through the Rockies, the Alaska Ferry north to Juneau and then fly over the coastal mountains to Atlin in a small plane."

I looked at him in disbelief, "you're kidding, right?"

Peter just gave me his full-on stare and smiled right into my face, with a "I dare you."

May 29, 1996, on the bus: 7.00a.m.

So here I am on a Greyhound coach, heading to Jasper, after flying into Edmonton yesterday. The bus is practically empty. It's foggy and overcast, lending a dismal view of a flat uninteresting scene from the bus. We stop for 15minutes at a truck stop and then proceed on our mountain - less way. An English couple has asked if they can move to the front seat and the driver jokes with a dour face. "No! It's a $5.00 charge."

1.55p.m. I am now on the train. I have the compartment pretty much to myself, just eight of us in the whole carriage. The conductor tells me I can move around to a larger seat if I prefer, but I am very comfortable where I sit. We are restricted to this car and cannot go up to the dome or to the restaurant car, but a snack car has arrived and I am snacking on a pack of potato chips and a Coca-Cola. Apparently we are coming up to Mt. Robson in about half an hour. The train goes snail slow and the track sometimes carves its way through huge rocks of pink and grey granite. If I could open this window, I reckon could touch them. We have come through one tunnel so far and right now we are in dense forest. I look for animals but so far haven't seen any. The visitor centre said the bears are out, but only in the low valleys collecting berries. There have been thirty siting's on this track this week, two were at the town line of Jasper. Oh! I just saw two lovely enormous Elk and a river running down into a waterfall!

The Australian family on board (mother, father and two daughters) have just called out there is an Elk on our port bow!

We arrived in Prince George at 8.20p.m... We all have to get off here and spend overnight in Prince George. I am met by Adrienne from the Bed and Breakfast I have registered at. I thought we were very late, until Adrienne told me somewhere around Mt. Robson we advanced our watches by one hour. The Bed and Breakfast is a suburban bungalow and very well cared for and comfortable. Adrienne took me on a tour of Prince George, which has a population of 75,000 and its pride and joy is the two year old University of Northern British Columbia. The university has a current enrolment of 2200 and specializes in Forestry, Biology, Women and Native Studies. The town centre itself is called the "Bowl" because it is completely surrounded by a grade of urban sprawl. It looks very pretty from our perch up at the university, which sits on the rim of the bowl. We go to a grocery store where I buy fruit and candy for the train tomorrow, then home to the B&B. I sit a while and talk with Adrienne and her husband before taking a luxurious hot bath.

My room and bed are warm and comfortable and I soon fall asleep while trying to read a book on Alaska.

May 30th, 8.30a.m.

We're back on the train again. Adrienne and her husband delivered me back safely, after a delicious breakfast of Grapefruit, Strawberries, Melon, Honey Grape Nuts cereal and toast with homemade jam donuts and coffee. (And I ate it all).

We are the same fellows on board as yesterday with an additional two. An early animal siting saw a Black Bear on the side of the tracks, just five minutes after leaving town. People call out now whenever an animal is sited. "Black Bear on the right-look down!" it's just oceans of fun and I want to do this forever. I have just ordered from the steward, a coffee to go with my cookie. The Australians are very bouncy this morning, full of early morning chit chat, funny how four people can sound like six! They are from Perth and this is their ninth week of vacation, having been to Paris, Germany, Zimbabwe and Ireland. They are going to Vancouver then on to the Grand Canyon.

It's my birthday today and I have opened an envelope Marcelline had given me. She is the best daughter, so thoughtful with a keen sense of humour, I am blessed. The card is so cute and there is a bracelet. The card is addressed to "Flower child" and says if I get short of cash I can "sell the bracelet."
Newsflash: "Two bears in the meadow" and everyone on board has gone crazy with excitement, the two Australian girls are still saying "Aah." I see lots of broken and abandoned log cabins, I wonder if they were trappers or early settlers and ponder the thought temporarily of how I might go about buying one. Newsflash! Moose across the river.

I have met up with a charming lady and found a kindred spirit in Elisabeth, who is going to Smithers. She is the same age as me and spends her summers on fire watch towers. Such a person has the duty to look for fires from atop a fire lookout tower, spotting smoke from wildfires. These towers are used in remote areas, normally on mountain tops or high elevations that have a good view of the surrounding country.

We have moved to the rear of the coach to accommodate 29 children getting on the train. The conductor kindly invited us to go up to the dome, so we have sat up there for over two hours, before going to the restaurant to drink cups of coffee and eat cakes with the crew. At Smithers, I got off the train as Elisabeth wanted me to meet her daughter and adopted grand-daughter who hails from Peru. I shall miss Elisabeth's company, she is a tiny frail looking lady, but there is nothing frail about her. Working in a fire lookout tower in the middle of a wilderness area takes a hardy type of person indeed, one who is able to survive without any other human interaction. I have much respect for Elisabeth and wished she was my neighbour.

Now it's back to my original seat, the coach has become crowded and I see a Black Bear and two cubs on the starboard bow. We are now following the Skeena River, the scenery awesome and dramatic. We go from dense bush to rivers; we carve through mountains and rock, around ledges and over the dizzy heights of wooden trestles.

At 8.30p.m. I am ensconced in my hotel at Prince Rupert. It is an old building, but clean and my room overlooks the bay. I visit a nearby restaurant for supper and enjoy lamb souvlaki and coffee. All is well in the land of loaves and fishes at this hour.

May 31, 1996; Prince Rupert.

After an early shower, change of clothes and breakfast, I headed out to explore the town. Starting first at the visitor centre, I went on to the museum, then did a walking tour of the town going out to Car Bay and back into town to the main shopping centre. This appears to be a very depressed town, it is quite small, homes are run down and lots of men loitering on the streets. Running out of places to see I came back to my room, did laundry, dyed my hair and was generally very lazy. At supper time I finally found the Fish and Chips I have been lusting for and they were excellent. At 10.30p.m. it was still light outside and it was difficult falling asleep.

June 01, 1996; Alaska Ferry.

I arrived in good time at the ferry dock and boarding was quick and efficient. At Customs however I had to declare an orange I was carrying. It appears that citrus fruits are not allowed. I am told I must peel it before arriving in Juneau and throw away the peel, but if it had been a 'Sunkist' brand it would have cleared customs with no problem.

I am currently sitting on a recliner chair on the observation deck. I came straight up here as soon as I boarded and found all the other backpackers here. There are many Australians again, they get such long vacation time and they put it to good use. My therm-o-rest is set up on the chair but not as yet my sleeping bag. I have chosen to camp on this deck as is the custom for backpackers. Cabins are available for a price, but I do prefer to stay here, I'm afraid if I go inside for a single minute I will miss something of the staggering coastline, inquisitive person that I am. A man in the chair behind me, has however, set up his bed and is at this moment already asleep. We are now on Alaska Time which is two hours behind my watch, which is two hours behind Ontario time but the same as Alberta time and one hour ahead of Pacific Time which happens also to be Prince Rupert time, if you catch my drift! I am confused as to what the real time is and I'm not touching my watch again because it's going to change again from Juneau to Atlin. I leave Juneau at 4.00p.m and arrive in Atlin at 4.00p.m, so you go and figure it out; I am quite dizzy with it all.

I did have an ace of a spot here on deck and I say "did" because when I went to get coffee, two selfish buffoons parked their chairs directly in front of mine, so close in fact, one is actually touching mine. So now I look at the back of someone's fat head instead of miles of ocean and uninterrupted shoreline. There is empty space at my side, big enough for two chairs, but do you think they had the common decency to use them. I feel violated! One looks like Mo of the three stooges and just as ugly, the other tall and skinny, unshaven and unwashed. I suppose if I do say something they will say "sorry, I don't speaka ze eenglis." Right! I'm praying for rain and then they will get wet, because they are just outside of the roofed area. I'm paying this penalty for sinfully going to the cafeteria and having a coffee and Danish before taking a walk around the deck.
There is a huge panoramic lounge with airplane type seats and a large restaurant and another lounge with little booths. I flop down and sulk in my chair, the man behind me is still snoring badly and he has been thus since Prince Rupert. An announcement comes over the speaker we have just crossed the U.S./Canada border and a lighthouse passes by with a U.S. light on it. Oh! I can't believe it, the two walking abortions have just moved their chairs to my side and it has started to rain! There is a God after all and prayers do work! I try hard to hide the smile that goes clear across my chops. Also, the dear gentleman has woken from his slumber and is talking a mile a minute to his wife, but is suddenly drowned out by an old codger next to

him, snoring his head off! All the backpackers at the back are sleeping also, I'm starving hungry and there is no Mars Bar machine.

We have seen lots of fish swimming and surfacing alongside the ferry and my lady friend next to me thinks they were Dalls Porpoise and we also believe we saw about six Orcas.

We stop at Ketchikan to load and unload passengers and I have time to take a bus tour. It is a really interesting town, nestled into the side of a mountain and much of it on stilts built on landfill. On many roads, you have a clear view of the stilts below. Needless to say, the town is small, but very busy. Some of the original streets remain intact, with the width of just a single car. Everything the town needs has been brought in by barge and our guide tells us, that which is ordered on Tuesday arrives the following Saturday. Containers arrive six days each week. The shops are wonderful, many boutiques, lots of Russian dolls in shop windows and flowers, flowers everywhere. Streets are lined with mountain ash trees and are heavy just now with white spring blossom. Hibiscus shrubs abound in fluorescent orange and vivid pinks.
The lady next to me went ashore looking for booze, my how we all differ, she rushing off to buy liquor and me rushing off to find chocolate bars. Can you believe I didn't find one and now I'm going into withdrawal?

At 3.00p.m we leave Ketchikan for Wrangell and our estimated time of arrival is 8.30p.m. weather permitting, which right now is overcast and cool, but altogether comfortable here in our "solarium."

I have been trying to read a book by Daphne Du Maurier and struggle with it. I cannot seem to concentrate on it and find myself constantly drifting, gazing vacantly out to sea, only to turn back the pages to re-read them over again. At Wrangell, my boozy lady friend confronts me, silhouetted against the afternoon sun, "Why don't you come ashore?" she says, puffing a stubby brown cigar, "You're bored with Daphne anyway." She is short and rotund with a rosy complexion; her hair is black with short frizzy curls. "I laugh and throw my book down. I love this lady; she is all good humour and no nonsense, tells it like it is and says she is joy-riding, sailing up and down the coast just for the hell of it. Relieved for the distraction, I'm glad to head for the dock; we are joined by another couple and "Booboo" the couple's tiny poodle. We wander lazily through the small town and I search everywhere again for a Mars Bar but came up with nothing. I buy a fistful of garnets from children on the dock who were selling little puddles of them.

As dusk descends, it rains again, so I crawl into my sleeping bag. Heaters in the roof overhead send down warm rays, we all huddle together, cheek by jowl now, just one big cosy family. I fell asleep almost instantly, the ferry gently swaying as we plough through the waves, the steady drone of diesel, all so peaceful and calming. I hear in the recesses of my sleepy mind we are approaching Petersburg, it was late into the night and in my drowsy stupor I slept through the docking. I was chagrined when I did wake, as Caroline said it was an awesome sight, "Like sailing through a Christmas Tree" she said, as the ferry inched its way through the narrows and the green and red marker buoys. She said the ferry went super slow, sometimes making hairpin turns. Gee Darn! How could I fall asleep at a time like that, guess I have to do this trip again.

I was up at 5.10a.m, cleaned my teeth, brushed my hair, had a blueberry muffin and coffee and was ready for our landing at Juneau at 9.15a.m... A little girl behind me has just come over to show me her garnets, which she is polishing with a Kleenex.

The docking at Juneau is the storm after the calm, people going this way and that. I feel thrust onto shore and look around to get *my bearings. Since I am going to be in Juneau all day, I don't want to carry my backpack around. Being smart and wise, I find lockers and for a mere 25¢ park my heavy pack. I find a shuttle bus for $5 to take me downtown. The driver is rough, he has a long reddish grey beard and equally long hair tied back in a ponytail. We are ushered brusquely onto a rude bus and the doors slam shut as he grinds into gear. We jolt forward and I read the sign over his head, "Sit down, Shut-up and Hold-on!"*

Once at the town centre, I ask politely, "when does the bus return to the ferry dock?" (The airport is right next door to it). "I'm not going back" he spits, "the terminal is closed." My mind glazes over. What? Who? When? Say it isn't so! Now I'm entering a mild stroke of the brain and feel shaky. My whole world is at the terminal and it's closed? Until tomorrow? My plane leaves at 4.00p.m. today. It's funny how you can go from laid back in a foggy kind of daze one minute and then in a nano second to sheer panic. In a freak stricken state, I sprint to find the local tourist bureau, time is of the essence and I need my backpack now! I find the tourist information, where a lady takes an eternity to tell me she "thinks the ferry terminal closed after the ferry left", AND she doesn't have a telephone to call up and confirm this. She then sends her daughter to get a cell phone. After what felt like another eternity, the daughter came back and confirmed that the ferry terminal was closing. Yep! It closes in half an hour. Still in panic mode I rushed to find a taxi that can get me up there at once. One hour later I am back downtown with my backpack and $50.00 U.S. lighter for a cab fare. There goes all the U.S. cash I had. I have traveller cheques, but of course, it's Sunday and the banks are closed so I try a hotel. They want 40% exchange rate! Are they kidding me? I gave them a $20.00 cheque and they gave me $12.00 back. I don't think I like Juneau, it's too expensive. There is a fleet of cruise ships here also, it's like downtown Yorkville on Saturday afternoon. I find a hotel shuttle to take me back out of town, it's only $7.00 and I sit in the bus with two well-heeled couples who *could have just been shopping at Holt Renfrew, all suits and heels, perfumed hair and designer bags; I am sweating cobs, haven't showered in two days, my hair is stuck to my head and my pack is taking up too much room. They eye me with the air of dragonflies that have come upon a gnat. I feel malicious and insolent and stare them down with a "Well, betcha don't know how to paddle a canoe" glare.*

Finding the Wardair desk was another exciting adventure. Like anyone would in their right mind, I went to the airport and asked for the Wardair desk. I was sent back out of the terminal, down a gravel road, "past the white hanger to the maroon hanger." There, in a tiny office I found the lone "check-in" desk, one of those small black and metal utility desks found in warehouses. And since I had time to spare, I immediately went to find a chocolate bar and a pop to steady my nerves from all the frustration. They only sell pop in a vending machine. I put in 90¢U.S. and got back 65¢ U.S. and 10¢ Canadian and no pop! Is this a number four day? (I am absolutely superstitious, regarding the number four) I quickly added the date, (day plus month plus year), nope, it's a six. And just to add the crowning glory to the day, I decide to check the pictures in my camera and there are none. I have failed to load a film; all the pictures of dolphins and orcas are a non-item. Now I have to be relegated to the tales of a fisherman, "honestly, there was hundreds and they were this big!" I can see the disbelieving faces even now. It's clear I definitely have to do this trip again and get it right next time.

Eventually, the plane is ready for take-off. It is a small four seater and because I am the only paying passenger, I sit in the co-pilot seat and am given ear phones. In the back two seats are the pilots' wife and her friend. The friend is soon to be married and they have been shopping in Juneau for a wedding dress. The small plane is based in Atlin and the pilot points out aspects of the stunning view below as we drift up to the sky. We fly over

The Irene Glacier, up and over the snow clad mountains and the pilot points to the peak of Devils Claw, poking up high in the coastal range. We seem to be floating up here for a long time, but in reality only a couple of hours. Below us lays a barren land of snowy peaks, some that we almost seem to touch and for miles and miles nothing but snow, ice and mountains. Finally, in the distance, the pilot points to a small patch of milky turquoise, it looks like a jewel that has been set in a white pearl necklace. "That is Atlin Lake", he says, I narrow my eyes and peer deeply at its sparkling brilliance. As we close in on the lake, our plane banks heavily and we fly around in circles, a wing dips deeply to the lake. We are looking for customs in the form of a pick-up truck. Finally we see what looks like a toy truck, way down there by the shore and banking again, we straighten out for the landing.

No one is here to meet me, so the customs officer, sans any sort of official uniform, kindly drives me in his pick-up out to the Atlin Art Centre, my home for the next ten days.
Atlin Art Centre is run by Gernot Dick, an Austrian by birth, who is also an adventurer, wilderness guide and photographer, to name only a few of his many talents. There was no one at the centre when I arrived so I wandered the grounds. There were a few cabins, a pond, some ghostly looking pieces of art hung on trees and everywhere was quiet and forlorn. After about an hour, a blond youth appeared. This was Dimitri and he introduced himself as the guide and art teacher. He is Polish and comes from Warsaw. Gernot arrived soon after and was most upset that I had arrived to no reception, he was very concerned. Apparently he lives close by and hurried home speeding back with a bowl of beans and rice. Dimitri took me over to the supplies depot for more food, but I wanted only a coffee and some cookies, he brewed fresh coffee and before long I felt quite relaxed. I was then given a tour of the facilities and Dimitri explained that the cabins had been rented out over the winter and guests had trashed them. Gernot had

*been travelling from Toronto the past few days when part of the
Alaska Highway had washed out, causing him to make a 600
mile detour, consequently, he and Dimitri have been awash in
chores to ready the camp. This explains the present situation. So
we are three here at this time and Gernot introduces me to the
property in detail. There is 15 acres of wilderness in which he
has singlehandedly built; a sauna and hot tub, a wood workshop,
a painting studio and a smoker oven. He has also built a natural
pond close to the buildings. Pioneer tents dot the perimeter. We
hike a small distance along a gravel road to where Gernot is
building a huge permanent house for himself. He has towed all
the way from Toronto, the makings of an observatory, which
right now lays prostrate on a huge flat-bed trailer.*

*Next Dimitri leads a short hike along the mountain ridge; I peer
down at our 'base camp' where three tents have been set-up.
Dimitri has his own A-Frame lodge which perches on the edge
of the mountain and overlooks the lake. A nearby stream serves
as a refrigerator and keeps yogurt and beer cold. I'm offered
a glacier cooled beer and accept gratefully. We sit and talk by
the stream for an age, the evenings are long and light and I am
surprised to learn it is already midnight as I head back down
the mountain to my solitary cabin and a rustic bed.*

Atlin Art Centre, June 03, 1996:

*I have just climbed to a ridge on Teresa Mountain behind us
and am sitting on a ledge just above the tree-line. Hopeless
at climbing I think the folks in Whitehorse can hear my heart
thumping right now. As I perch on a rock I am surrounded by
a bevy of wild flowers. There are wild Lupines, but I have to
research white flowering shrubs for their names, could they be
Labrador Tea? When I get my breath back I will take a picture
of them, in the meantime I'm getting dizzy when I look down.*

This morning I went into Atlin with Gernot and Dimitri. It is an earthly little paradise that sits snug against the shore of Atlin Lake. There are two stores, a post office is in someone's home and all buildings are built of logs. There are four cabins at the water's edge, deserted and ready to be claimed by whoever wants them. Atlin was once a major gold mine town and there are the remains of mines in the area that are still staked.

The afternoon is spent in lazy contemplation and I park myself by the pond. When I look into the water I have the sensation of floating and drifting on the air, as the wind sends tiny ripples past me. The pond is fed from a spring up the mountain and has been cleverly tapped into with unobtrusive pipes that are hidden in the landscape. All is silent save for the trickle from the spring and the birds singing in the trees. Everywhere deserted and still, I bask in the peaceful solitude; Gernot and Dimitri have returned to Atlin to pick up two more guests.

Kristin and Elaine will be my two soul mates for the next ten days. Dimitri takes us to our new home, a campsite on the other side of the road and over a rocky ridge. By the time we have climbed over the ridge I can hardly speak. Hopefully, after ten days of this I will breeze over.
Three tents are set-up, mine is blue and nestles at the foot of a high rock face, Elaine is further away in a yellow tent and Kristin nestled in another direction in a green tent. We are not visible to each other, so one has the feeling of camping alone. At 7.00p.m. we all congregate in the main building and are introduced to our cook for the week. We meet Jane, an academic from Kentucky and she speaks with that slow pleasant southern drawl. I'm guessing in her early sixties, she is tall and slim with blond hair. Elaine comes from Prince William, married with two children and in her early thirties, she is poised and soft spoken; this is her her third visit to Atlin. Kristin is the same age as Elaine, is a Laboratory Technician from Vancouver, of

medium height with a short round figure; she has more trouble than I when climbing the ledge.

Back at the main cabin, the table setting for supper lends a cosy ambience and we feast on vegetable stew with sour cream, red wine and pecan pie. Gernot talks about the trips he has planned and gives a slide show of his many photographs. Many are taken with a huge zoom lens, there are pictures of the flowers that flourish here, with many zoomed in close-ups, such as an ant sitting on a dandelion petal. He talked about looking at lines and tension points, of form in Art and Photography and stressed the importance of light and shade. I have to admit, some of it left me in a dark shade and it was slightly over my head at times, but he is a very patient teacher and does not mind at all repeating things over and over. I'm hoping some of it will 'sink' in.

June 4th, 1996: Pioneer Creek:

We hiked all day today, following the Pioneer Creek. It went up into the mountains first, following an alpine meadow, then down to the river until we found ourselves in a canyon. The creek at the bottom of the canyon was in a hurry and birds were surfing downstream at a ferocious rate. We came across two trapper cabins and evidence of gold mining in the area, silt beds, a post showing a claimed stake and many holes, which Gernot said would be dug by gold-diggers testing the soil. Some huts were built into the mountainside and we found the foundations of a cabin complete with an outhouse just five feet away. A rusted pot belly stove and a decaying rubber boot were just some of the remains abandoned there. Another cabin still in pretty good shape was just big enough for a bunk bed and a pot belly stove, both still there.

The climb back out of the canyon was very steep and a grassy spot at the top of a waterfall provided the perfect place for a picnic stop of fresh bread, cheese and brownies.

June 5th, 1996; 6.08p.m.

I am somewhere on the shore of Atlin Lake, we canoed two hours to this spot and will camp here for two days. Our transport is voyageur canoes, of which there are two, meaning three to a canoe. Gernot, Jane and Elaine are in one and Dimitri, Kristin and myself in the other. Our canoes where heavily laden with tents, stoves and provisions, which we spent all morning packing. For dinner tonight we have; baked potatoes, chicken, broccoli, Beer and chocolate mousse. Breakfast tomorrow is pancakes and Red River. Lunch will be Tuna Salad; fresh bread and cream cheese. Tomorrow night it's spaghetti and meat sauce, wine and salad. Gernot is not going to see us hungry. We also are carrying cookies, coffee, herbal tea, hot chocolate and marshmallows. The bread is from Whitehorse, homemade baguettes and so delicious. We have five loaves plus a huge slab of cheese, trail mix and apples for snacks.

After supper tonight there will be a workshop on Mark Making, a form of sketching apparently, which proves to be closing your eyes and scribbling at random on a blank sheet. Gernot produces brilliant abstract works, mine is merely childish scribble.

We are surrounded by enormous snow-capped mountains and are camped in a sheltered bay. The lake is a deep turquoise and very calm right now. Atlin is often referred to as "little Switzerland" and right now I can see why. Jane and Kristin have just taken some beer from the lake and I am going to find a cooler place to sit. I have just finished my first real sketch and it is crap.

Diane Campbell Thompson

June 6th, 1996.

We are back in our canoes again for a trip across the lake to an old railway bed trail. The rails were set-up during the gold rush days to transport logs. It was a flat and easy three mile walk through the bush and again there is much evidence of settlers and gold miners. Most of the railway ties are now covered in moss and decayed, but we each found a couple of good spikes for souvenirs. At the trail end we find the remains of the old train; pieces of ceramic dishes and coloured glass from bottles which all sit in shallow water. We picked up many pieces for Gernots museum and he found a large part from the train, which he is taking back to use as a planter. Petou, who is Gernots tiny Jack Russell dog, is having great fun diving into the surrounding bush, but whenever he runs to walk by our side, we know a Grizzly is nearby. We have seen them from our canoe and Gernot carries a small fire cracker which he will release if we are confronted.

Gernot brought a photograph from his collection; it was of a leaf, magnified many times. Our project was to go out and find it. We found it difficult, being so enlarged, but eventually Kristin, Elaine and I found it. It was from the soapberry bush, so named by the Indians, because it froths up like soap when mashed together.

We had another sketching lesson, this time with Dimitri and it seemed in no time at all, Jane and Gernot called us for dinner. The evening was spent talking around a glowing fire, another lesson on mark making and then more idle talk until finally going to bed at 2.00a.m. still in day-light.

June 7th, 1996.

We were dared today to jump in the lake and Kristin and I took up the challenge. These lakes are glacier fed and while they look inviting are exceedingly cold. The rule was we had to be deep enough to get our hair wet. Forget about cold, think frigid; think ICE! Feet and legs immediately go numb and forget about even trying to swim. It was breathtaking, literally, but won us both a T-Shirt of the Art Centre.

We are hiking again today, but not too far, exploring only the forest. We had a photography lesson and I photographed small things, lichen on rocks, little puddles of water, trying to find "light and shade" and "form." We posed as a group for brochures and web pages for the centre and watched a black bear and her cinnamon coloured cub eating in the bush. The mom seemed not at all interested in us but kept right on eating.

We are currently waiting on the shore to canoe back home, but the water is too rough and we have to wait for calmer weather. It is 6.43p.m. and the trip back will be about two hours, I hope tomorrow is a rest day.

June 10th, 1996:

We are presently lazing in a lagoon off Atlin Lake. We have just come to the end of two gruelling days and right now enjoying some peaceful rest. Elaine is painting, Dimitri is fishing, Gernot and Jane are sleeping and Kristin is quietly staring meditatively at the lake.

Friday last, was gruelling. Ploughing our way back home across the windy choppy lake, felt like canoeing through mashed potatoes. We kept an eye on the point as we tried to round it into Atlin, but no matter how long and hard we paddled, the point never moved. Eventually, to our complete and utter relief, we beached our canoes and Gernot hurried straight over to hug each of us saying how proud of us he was. He said the residents of Atlin would have been looking out of their windows at us and saying "are zay going out, or are zay coming in, yah!" We fell to the sand in a mix of giddy giggles and utter exhaustion.

Last Saturday, we had a free day and Elaine and I climbed Monarch Mountain at 4300 ft. It took us about three hours to reach the top and the trees changed as we climbed, going from fir to poplar and willow and then to no trees. Lots of forget-me-nots and anemone's sprinkled the mountainside and at the very top a small ice-field to navigate, with knee-deep snow. At the top the wind was strong and icy cold, I watched briefly a small plane flying below us before we hurried back down.

Sunday we left for Cathedral Mountain, again by canoe, but the lake was so rough we had to take shelter on an island and call for help to take us back. We were picked up by Archie with his tug-boat and had to trail our two canoes behind.

Prior to this, Gernot had fixed a motor to his canoe and towed our canoe behind him, but again it got too rough and we were forced to make a hasty camp. With no time to erect tents, we slept under the stars. He also forgot the propane for the stove so we had hot cider over a fire then crawled into our bags for the night. We were up at 5.00 a.m. and continued in tow up to Cathedral Mountain. Even with the motor, we still had to paddle, we were beating into a head wind the whole time and everyone was getting extremely tired and irritable. The oars of the voyageur are big and heavy and the canoe so cumbersome, our arms were ready to fall off. We made a short lunch stop and Jane seems unhappy, left us at dinner to go into her tent. Dimitri and Kristin went Cray fishing and Jane just unzipped her tent and yelled, "Would ya'all be quiet when you come back!"

June 11th, 1996:

Last night, being very tired, I went to bed at 9.30p.m. I was soon joined by Kristin and Elaine; we lie awake talking over the day and the lessons regarding the art in nature. One thing that was emphasized constantly is we should take note of nature's habit of similarity without repeats. For example, all the trees of the forest look similar, but no two are exactly the same. We laughed and guffawed as I pointed to our three bodies, laying side by side like sardines in a tin, we were a living example of "Similarity without repeats" I smirked and we giggled like school girls. Jane called from her tent "would you all be quiet and ya'all have the time?" We sunk deeper into our bags and tried ever so hard to hide our school girl giggles.
Next morning, Gernot made wry comments about our conversation last evening and of our making fun of "nature's habits" assuring us, with a big smile, he had heard every word.

Jane, who was hired as cook, is tired today and feels she is doing too much work so we must each make our own lunch today; I opted to make myself a sausage sandwich and coffee. Elaine and Dimitri went for a hike, Kristin has gone for a nap and Gernot has gone after Elaine and Dimitri with Petou. I turned my talents to washing the dishes and putting them away and tidying the food box. Jane has begun to carry everything down to the shore for loading into the canoes, but when Gernot comes back, he says we may have to linger here until after the dinner hour, so everything must be brought back up again. We spied another Black Bear walking along the shore across from our camp site.

Diane Campbell Thompson

June 12th, 1996.

I'm perched on a very rocky island, it's 10.34 a.m. and we are again shipwrecked! Well, not shipwrecked exactly, more like castaways. We were all up and ready to leave at 7.30 a.m. making two valiant attempts at crossing the lake to go home, but no luck. The water looks calm until we came out of the inlet and a strong westerly almost upset us. We pulled off to some rocks and climbed up to get a better view of the water, then climbed back down to make another attempt, this time using the motor, but the waves and high wind drove us back again. We wait now for Archie and his tug-boat again, but he may not be here until tomorrow.

We settle down to amuse ourselves, collecting stones, sketching and mark making. Jane has made pretty wind chimes using large nails and pebbles found on the beach.

When we do get back to the Art centre, it is the end of our trip; we pack our bags and make ready to leave. I am taking a small bus to Whitehorse where I plan to spend a few days, before taking another Greyhound bus to Edmonton.

The Atlin Art centre leaves me with a rich treasure box of memories, my fellow campers Elaine and Kristin have made it so. Jane has kept me happy and well fed. The lessons I take away from the sensitive and erudite teachings at the Atlin Art Centre have added a new and wider dimension to my thoughts.

Hunting on Westchester Hill

*It is 4.00 p.m. on Westchester Hill, Richie left at about 3.10 p.m.
to hunt again. I felt a tad guilty for not going with him again,
but I feel quite lazy and the thought of tramping back out of the
woods in the dark just slays me. I am out of shape and I huff
and puff over deadfall, unbroken paths and rocks, it's not as if it
was a trail. One gets hit in the eye with branches or poked in the
back of the head, plus I have to wear a hat and that makes me so
hot. We have to wear camouflage orange; I have an old orange
vest and hat that belonged to Richie. We sit in the stand for two
hours and see absolutely nothing. A crow passed over a few
times; he seemed riled about something for he was squawking
his head off. I am amazed how still the forest is; nothing seems
to be going on. No birds singing, no squirrels, no chipmunks, no
deer and thankfully, no bear. Richie says he saw a squirrel and
sees deer all the time apparently. Probably at the apples he laid
out, usually a doe and two fawns, I would like to have seen that.
I sit on an old upturned bucket, Richie is on an old kitchen chair,
we sit way up in the branches, all decked out in camouflage and
hidden behind a camouflage net. Thank goodness the weather is
good and not too cold, for we cannot move a hair. Richie says I
can only move my eyeballs! Needless to say the circulation stops
in my backside and my feet slowly turn to ice, then my hands. I
was so happy when he gave the sign to leave, we communicate
up here in sign language and it's all very solemn. Then down
we go, the gun goes first, then Richie climbs down two rungs,
then I step out onto the lower branches. Richie is the perfect
gentleman and stays close to me as I climb slowly down. I can't
help wandering though, about him peeing at the base of the tree.
Isn't that sort of marking your territory? Don't all animals have
a strong sense of smell? Do you think they might know we are
there and that is why we don't see anyone? I'm no hunter but it
seems that could be a reason.*

The first time I went hunting with Richie was quite an education for me. I am not from a family of hunters; the only hunting I have ever done is for a bargain in the mall and we buy all our meat at the supermarket.

We left on the ATV, Richie decked out in camouflage from head to toe. When we arrived at the 'place' he jumped off the machine, pulled his mask over his face and grabbing his rifle, beckoned me to follow. He looked like a terrorist.

Quietly and solemnly we walked in single file through thick brush, coming to stop behind a couple of trees. Stationing me close to him, he beckoned me with a finger to his lips to keep quiet and pointing to a small stream ahead of us, he whispered, "they" (the Deer) "will come to the stream to drink."

Surely, I thought, he can't be serious. You mean to tell me that when Bambi's dad comes down for a drink he will shoot him? It's not fair and it's unjust.

We stood there for I don't know how long and all the time I pray that no Deer will come and they don't.

So great, I'm happy and we head back to the road and I tell Richie, "If a Deer had come to that little brook, I would have had the biggest coughing fit of my life."

"Then I would have shot you" he says calmly.

Anyway, I'm glad I stayed in the cabin today, I can see the traffic down on the Cobequid pass; the sun is dropping and the distant black hills are turning pink. Behind me through the trees the horizon has turned to orange. I have lit the oil lamp by which I now write, a candle glows in the window and I have put two logs on the fire. Two potatoes are nestling in the embers; we will eat them smothered with butter at supper time with some nice cooked venison. (Yes I know what you are saying, oh the fickle hearted.... but I do like the taste of venison!)

Richie will be home about 6.00p.m. then we shall eat. Afterward I may have a little Rye and Ginger, we will play a game of cards and I will get whopped again. The scene is one of simple unparalleled peace and in the world of loaves and fishes all is well.

Becoming an Outdoor Woman (BOW Weekend)

*H*ere I go on this the first day of my BOW weekend. I first found out about this course from Flo in New Brunswick who was an instructor. When I saw the display at the outdoor show I immediately signed up. It's all about learning outdoor skills and is a women only event taught primarily by women. The range of subjects offered is mind boggling, e.g. Animal Tracking; Canoeing; Camping; Moose Ecology; Map and Compass; Archery; Muzzle Loading; Knots: Wilderness Survival, to name only a few! I plan to take:-

Introduction to Firearms

Map and Compass

Rifle Shooting

Chainsaw

I left Cobourg at 8.00a.m. and had a pleasant uneventful drive north along Highway 35. I should have stopped to take a picture of this road as it is the same route I took to the Minden Sled Dog races last winter. Then the road was a study in white, the trees laden with snow and the snow banks piled high on either side. Today everywhere is lush and green and the trees are a profusion of spring buds. All the lakes are free of ice and a deep indigo blue. The sky is overcast but no rain as of yet. I play my Suzanne Chiani music which always puts me in a northern state of mind and dream of buying a cottage up here. I love the quiet places and Minden or Bancroft would suit me fine. At Minden I get out for a stroll along the main street and stop in a restaurant for coffee and a muffin. I also visited the information centre and came out laden with books, maps and brochures.

The Leslie Frost Centre is a hive of activity when I arrive just before noon. Lots of women here already, some in groups or pairs and some like me alone. We are bunked in dormitory style rooms that sleep two and I am assigned Block 70 Room 7. Despite the fact it sounds like a prison address, the whole place is warm and inviting. Pristine clean and bright, our rooms have large windows that overlook the grounds. The building is only two storeys high and very long; our rooms seem to be all on the ground floor. I am sharing with a young woman of about 25 who hails from Ajax. She is with several other friends who are billeted further along the hallway. Our room has two single beds, each with a bedside cabinet and lamp. There is a large washroom and showers are down the hall.

After a brief reception and welcome lecture we race off to lunch in the dining hall. Seating is arbitrary and meals are buffet style. Today we have Boiled Cod; Meatballs and noodles; Lots of salad and fresh bread, Juices, Coffee and Tea. Then there is a huge table of deserts. However, we cannot linger long as our first class starts at 1.00 p.m. sharp and I rush up the stairs for my first firearms class.

We are a class of about eight women and three instructors, two of whom are female. Laid out on the desks are various rifles and already I am feeling a tinge of excitement mixed with apprehension. Guns and rifles seem to represent a dreadful power. We first must learn firearm safety and each in turn learns how to disarm a gun, then how to load it. We practice on the various 'actions' e.g., Pump; Semi-automatic (or self-loading) and Bolt Action. We inspect different types of bullets and touch on projectiles. We were all so absorbed in our subject that we failed to notice the time, 5.30 p.m. – dinner hour and time to eat again! Entering the dining room we are met with the delicious smells of Poached Salmon, Chicken Cacciatore, every kind of vegetable and salad plus the now 'de rigour' dessert table.

After supper there is a presentation in the auditorium on "A Year in the Life of a Deer." After this we have a choice of more seminars and I opt for Fur Grading. This was a presentation from one of only two fur houses in the province and there were trunks full of hides just as they are received from the trappers. On display was Beaver; Fisher, Ermine, Wolf, Marten (Sable) and Raccoon amongst many more. We listened as we were told how the pelts are graded; checking for signs of battles where the hide would have scars or bites, making it less valuable. An especially interesting fur was one that had been knitted into a stylish hat.

All weekend long there are classes morning and afternoon. Saturday morning found me tramping through the bush with map and compass for orienteering class, it poured with rain but I didn't get lost to my eternal pride, however one body did and while we ate lunch a search party was at work. Afternoon our class of eight were driven to an open range a few kilometres from the centre. After tramping through long grass we were positioned on a short rise. Our teachers now are Olympic skeet shooters. Wow!

We each are handed a rifle, mine a "pump action - 20gauge Browning." As an instructor fires the skeet from a point to our left, we trace its flight through the air, aim and shoot. One lady breaks down in tears; she is afraid to hold the gun and cannot think about shooting. The instructor's cradle her in their arms, reassure, gently talk and she foregoes her turn. Now it's up to me, I am really quite nervous, there's a sinking feeling in my stomach and my mouth is dry. Carefully I raise the barrel, I'm shaking a little and I'm afraid of the 'kick back,' which is the point when the gun is fired and it rebounds back into your shoulder with such force it can be extremely painful. I'm shown how to brace my shoulder and suddenly I hear someone shout "FIRE!" and there is no time for nerves, all of a sudden the skeet is airborne and I'm following its flight, I fire and ……..miss. Two more skeet's are released in quick succession and with each one I gain more confidence, now it's all about aim, who mentioned 'kick back,' I'm too engrossed in hitting my target and this game has become all absorbing. The whole episode can only have lasted three minutes, but my pulse has quickened, I feel powerful and controlling. The gun was easier to handle than I thought, I love this sport of skeet shooting, I'm proud of my gun. We each rotate shooting practice and the distressed lady has been persuaded to at least hold her gun. Before we leave in the late afternoon she will fire three shots through tears of joy and liberation.

Sunday morning is spent with a chain saw. Decked out in chain saw pants, steel toe boots, helmet and goggles we industriously spend the morning from swinging an axe to cutting logs with a chain saw. Making and splitting logs we are girls doing guy things and loving it.

Sadly all good things must come to an end and so it happens with this weekend. I take home a new feeling of self-worth, a confidence not felt before. Living alone as I do, it gives me comfort to know that I can take care of myself. I have never wanted to rely on someone else for my existence, or take care of me; I want to take charge of my own destiny. To make my own choices in this world, to make my own mistakes in this one shot we get here on earth and not as I take my last breath realise I had let others dictate my path. Maybe it is simply a rebellious reaction from childhood. I remember so often I was told "no, you can't" when I so wanted to try. "No you can't take horse riding lessons, no you can't join the Girl Guides, no you can't join the Girls Life Brigade, no you can't be a teacher and no you can't stay at school longer." I struggle and sink with dominance and strive to stay afloat. Here, amongst women I was able to try those experiences that beguiled but were considered too rough for the gentler sex. To push out my boundaries and test my capabilities I seem to be ever drawn to. It's me, it's what I do best and I like it and thrive there. Being a single divorced woman now, with children who have flown the nest, it is up to me alone now to forge ahead with a new life. Like waves washing against the shore, my feelings of self-worth come crashing home only to ebb and flow back again. Hopefully my tide will slowly rise and my harbour of content will be filled.

CHILKOOT TRAIL, ALASKA

The infamous Chilkoot Trail starts in Dyea Alaska and was originally a Tlingit trail over the coastal mountains. During the Klondike gold rush, two trails led to the Klondike; the White Pass out of Skagway or the Chilkoot Pass out of Dyea. The White Pass was deceptive, appearing to be easier than the high Chilkoot. But it quickly gained a dark reputation for sharp rocks, mud, slime and slippery precipices. So many horses died on this trail that history has re-named it the Dead Horse Trail. Horses were mired in mud, urged along by constant flogging, overloaded, starved and it has been said, some actually committed suicide by throwing themselves over the cliffs. The trail soon became impassable and as the stampeder's came to a halt, men turned to the dizzy heights of the Chilkoot Pass as a way to the gold mines of the Yukon. The Chilkoot trail is 33 miles long and dubbed the "meanest 33 miles in history." Following at first the Dyea River in the peaceful Dyea valley, it then winds up and through rich rain forest before arriving at the base of the coastal mountains. Rising thirty five hundred feet above Dyea, the mountains command respect and dread. In August 1997, with my then partner, we decided to hike the trail on the 100th anniversary of the Klondike Gold Rush. This is my journal of that trail.

Sunday: August 24th, Whitehorse:

After driving from Ontario for eight days, we arrived in Whitehorse yesterday (Saturday) in rain. I always feel I have come home when I enter Whitehorse, there is a quiet that settles over this city that feels peaceful, nestled as it is in this valley, surrounded by golden peaks. The Robert Service camp ground is OK, but a little cramped and we feel like foreigners amongst the throngs of German campers. It looks like most of them are on the water as I see lots of wet gear hanging out to dry. After making our camp 'ship shape and Bristol fashion' we go into town to the T&M lounge to listen to some local bands. It's a warm and friendly place with good music and Rye and Gingers (TM size).The seats are cosy sofas and armchairs, the lights are dim, a Bar runs along one wall and pool tables occupy one corner.

This morning we set out to explore Miles Canyon. The Yukon River rounds a bend there and it is surrounded on all sides by high cliffs. The rock cliffs tower high above the river, which races through in a noisy blue green bubbling and gurgling ribbon. We took the hiking path signed "Canyon City" which hugged the river, sometimes rising high on the cliffs then dropping back to the river banks. The views were magnificent, Jack Pines in the forest, Juniper and soap berry bushes. Lupines were not in flower but lots of lichen in bright orange, pale green, white and black on the rocks and boulders. I see also lots of orange on the canyon walls.

Back into town we checked out the McBride Museum, watching a long video about the Yukon, checking out Sam Magee's Cabin and a working model of a sluice box. Also went to the Harvest fair down by the SS Klondike. There was local entertainment; children singing, prizes for the best vegetable, best knitting, best needlepoint, best quilting. There is talent here I tell you, quilts made by 13 year olds put most of us to shame.

Tonight's supper was hot dogs, macaroni and cheese, pasta salad, vanilla pudding and coffee. I broke down and had two Caramilk bars and a coke over a roasting camp fire. We tried our hand at the communal wood pile, I half cut through a piece, BJ took over and went on a marathon, cutting everything in sight, so much so we had to get the car from the parking lot to carry it all back to our site. Think he was trying to outdo four German campers who earlier chopped and hauled an armful. A squirrel is presently calling for help as a dog is standing under the tree waiting to have some fun but the squirrel has work to do. I tried to intercept but the dog insists on playing with the squirrel and not me.

Earlier this morning while cooking breakfast, our campsite became a war zone. The squirrel sat at the top of a pine tree throwing cones down, they were falling like bombs, to the left to the right, on top of the tarp. It was almost a danger zone. After he had stripped the tree bare of cones, he ran at breakneck speed carrying the cones to his cache two sites away. It was like watching "Beat the Clock" where you had to get as many groceries as you could before the bell rang.

A backpack has washed up on the shore of the river by our campsite; it's an external frame containing a poncho, a tea infuser, three plastic bowls, a rock sliced in two with something inside too rotten and soggy to identify, two army belts, two topographical maps, one of Whitehorse, the other of Lake Laberge, two excellent fishing reels, a box of lures and itinerary (handwritten in German) and a large plastic container with miscellaneous items stamped "made in Germany." Its loss must have caused a problem for whoever lost it, but looking at the water, I would not be surprised to know many a pack has gone the same way. The river boils like a kettle and even though we are far back from the Yukon's banks, the sound of rushing water can be loudly heard. It sounds lovely when you are snug in your sleeping bag at night.

Monday, August 25th, Carcross:

We drove to Atlin today under warm sunny skies. The road is mostly mud and gravel and the scenery spectacular. Yukon Mountains reach up to the clouds, looking as is made of pure granite; others are covered in pines from top to bottom. They all dip down to blue green lakes. We had lunch in Atlin and went over to visit Gernot, but he was at Ruby Mountain with guests and so I showed BJ the ridge where I camped, the hot tub, the fish house, the man-made pond and the prospector tents. We started the climb up Monarch Mountain but only gained the first ridge before turning back.

Tuesday, August 26th, Skagway:

We were up early and off in a steady rain and had to pack everything wet! It rained all the way to Skagway, but the steep descent into Skagway was breath-taking. Huge mountains of granite, moss covered boulders, waterfalls and raging rivers. We stopped to look down on Dead Horse Gulch and espy the remains of the White Pass route across the gulch. I feel a sense of foreboding as I survey the land. It looks desolate, intimidating, the boulders look obstinate and mean and they are many. It looks a hostile land.

At the ghostly remains of Dyea were piles of rotting timbers lying prostrate and moss covered in the misty rain forest. Everywhere is wet, there's a hush in the air, only the sound of rain dripping off tree branches. And there in the middle of the forest, the slide cemetery with 70 graves. Many stampeders died in an avalanche, their headstones a rude wooden stake, with the words "Died in an avalanche April 3, 1898." One alone amongst the markers read "shot accidentally on the mountain."

From the cemetery we headed to the Rangers office to collect our permits and sign-in on U.S. Customs. Our permits are like ski tags and we have three, one each, plus one for camping. These must be visible on our packs at all times. We were given a warning also of a bear at Linderman City and will only be allowed to advance from there in parties of six or more.

After picking up rail tickets for the descent back down we strolled the streets of Skagway. The town is recreated as it was in 1898, with wooden sidewalks, old buildings, saloons and stores etc. There are three cruise ships in the harbour and pretty girls dressed in period costumes drive flocks of tourists to and from the dock in horse drawn carriages or elongated old fashioned buses. Skagway belongs to a scant few of us and sits in peaceful silence once the cruise ships leave and the stores close. The town sits nestled at the foot of huge mountains and a glacier can clearly be seen sliding down a vast slope. We are camped tonight in Skagway at a pleasant camp site and I have just come back from a refreshing shower. We have spent the afternoon preparing for tomorrow, putting packs together and clothes laid out for the trek. At the rangers office we were shown a video of the trail and we both wonder quietly if we are in our right mind. It looks simply awful, to say nothing of the scales which look nothing less than dreadful! Fog, rain, mud, bears, brute cold, a 45° climb, rope bridges, God! What a mess it is.

Wednesday, August 27th, Canyon City: 3.00p.m.

We made an early start this morning and were on the trail at 9.00a.m. Met lots of people, about 24, along the way, many Germans again, a party of four in their 20's, a father and son duo, three men travelling solo, one couple (who are camped here for the night also) and another young couple who have gone on to Sheep Camp. Rangers keep track of hikers and no more than 60 are allowed to be on the trail at any one time.

The trail at first was exceedingly steep. The guide book said the first quarter mile is an initiation, being straight up and they were seriously right. We moved slowly, huffing and puffing like two old steam engines. At mile three we saw the remains of an old saw mill, a rusty kitchen sink and some old Hills Bros. coffee cans. We travelled mostly through rich rainforest; everything is covered in moss, the rocks and the trees, the logs strewn everywhere and even branches. I think I have seen every variety of mushroom that ever poked its head up through the brown earth; red, black, yellow, maroon, brown, white, pink, spotted, plain, umbrella, flat, upside down, laced, pancake, big, small and these are just the ones on the ground. I could write a eulogy on the ones growing on the trees, some look like bright white clumps of corral. We stopped at Finnegan's Point for our first rest break. The Taiya River is almost always at our side. It rages noisily down and its roar can be heard even from inside the warm-up cabin. BJ has filtered our water and also some extra bottles for a German couple who have been drinking straight from the river. Egad!

There have been lots of little bridges crossing creeks and rivers on the way and a cool refreshing waterfall that I dipped my toes into. It was ice cold and I couldn't bear the chill for long, but it did wonders for burning sore skin.

It has taken us six hours to get here to Canyon city where there is a large log cabin in which we can get warm and cook a meal. There is a pioneer stove with lots of wood stacked beside it and it feels cosy and welcoming. There are lots of people here, but most just passing through on their way to Sheep Camp. We have made coffee and as my feet are very sore already, I wear sandals. The sun is shining directly on the cabins porch and I am enjoying this quiet interlude to write my journal. Sightseeing planes and helicopters hover above, BJ is chewing the fat with a lady from Florida. Someone said tomorrow is an easy trek, just two hours.

Thursday, August 28th, Sheep Camp: 5.00p.m.

We are so lucky with the weather so far, this trail would be the pits in the rain. We left at 9.00a.m. this morning and it has taken us 6 hours to get here. So much for the soothsayers promising an easy hike. It has been a hard day with some very steep ascents only to descend steeply down again into what is called "gulches." We crossed several bridges again, over rivers and creeks, even crossing the Taiya River. At Sheep Camp the river is about one hundred feet from the shelter cabin and has picked up speed. It is boisterous and hurling itself down the mountainside. Sitting on the rocky bank one has to shout to be heard. The glacier I saw from Canyon city is more prominent now. To the north sit two enormous mountains, mostly granite and we are wondering if the pass goes by or over them. We cannot see traces of the pass from here, mercifully, for I think it would make me feel faint. We seem to have merged into a six - some, with Brigitte and Erik (from Germany.) Brigitte now lives in Key Largo and she has given me her card. We have swapped addresses and promise to keep in touch. I am full of admiration for Brigitte, she is probably in her sixties, Blond, medium height, well-built mature figure. She insists on ambling slowly and appears to handle the terrain all in her good natured and steady stride. Erik looks much younger and now lives in Norway; he does not speak English. His youthful stride takes no apparent effort. The other couple keep pretty much to themselves. He is ex-army, wears army fatigues, is slim and of medium build, with gray hair, a well preserved 58 years young is my guess. She is late teen or early twenties, slim, quiet, shoulder brown hair. He refers to her as his wife.

BJ has filtered six bottles of water (two for Brigitte and Erik) and I cooked a Rice Pilaff for supper. I ate a full bag of trail mix on the way plus half of a power bar so I'm not so hungry tonight. I'm tired after such a rough day; we took much longer than we thought we would. So many climbs; boulders, tree roots and mud. According to history, the stampeders called this the worst part of the trail; I reserve my judgement until the end. The flies are miserable, persistent little blighters that bite and draw blood. The cursed prickly Devils Club lines the trail on both sides to add misery to injury.

We took a side trail over to the original Canyon City site. A huge boiler, a broken down cabin and cast iron stove sit choking in tall grass and weeds. Lots of pans and buckets, rusted and rotten with age lay strewn about the ground. I simply cannot imagine carrying a stove up here. It's a nightmare come true just to lug my backpack.

Tomorrow they tell us to allow 10 hours to reach Happy Camp. It's the day of the big climb. I live in part dread, part excited anticipation. I think we will make many stops.

Saturday, August 29th, Linderman City:

I did not write my journal yesterday, much too exhausted. We got to camp in the dark at 9.00 p.m. thoroughly exhausted and BJ feeling ill. His hips are sore and he is limping badly. My feet were blistered and the soles so sore it was painful just to stand up. Add on a splitting headache, backache and shoulders screaming from strap abuse by my pack. Both of us are feeling nauseous. It took everything BJ had to put up the tent. There was a strong cold wind that came howling from the coast and over the mountains. I insisted anyway that we both eat something as neither of us had eaten since breakfast and our water stops at the end were too far apart. That was my fault, I was anxious to get to camp before dark. I made us Hot Chocolate and soup by flashlight in the warm-up cabin and by 10.00 p.m. we literally collapsed into our sleeping bags.

We started out at 7.40a.m. and hit Happy Camp at 9.00p.m. 13.5 hours with few rest stops. It was without a doubt, the toughest day. The evening before the Ranger had talked to us all, about weather and bears. Both reports were good, she said it is very rare to have sun and clear skies on the summit, but thank heaven for small mercies, that's what we had. She also said the Bear that had been a problem at Bear Loon Lake had been shot, but we must still check with the Ranger there and we still must leave in parties of no less than six.

The trail from Sheep Camp is virtually a goat path. It starts climbing immediately and never stops. Initially we climbed along the side of a waterfall, all the way from bottom to the top of it. It was extremely taxing and we stopped several times for water. Next the trail led us to a huge rock slide and then we were climbing boulders. At first we could see tiny Inuksuk's to follow and then we lost them so stopped to read the guide, which said, in the absence of markers, stay close to the river, which we did. But after some time, BJ spotted a trail below us. Obviously we had strayed quite a way from the path, so there was nothing to do but crash through the brush. Lucky that BJ saw this, or we would have climbed those stupid boulders into eternity. While descending, I managed to lose my footing and fell, smack down in the middle of a patch of Devil's Club. It is an aromatic shrub being densely covered with spines and prickles. Standing 1 - 3 m (occasionally as high as 5 m) and I know first-hand that it is indeed covered with spines and prickles. BJ had to yank me out and all I could do was yell "Quick, get me out, get me out." It must have looked hilarious. Next was the 'Scales' and of course, it is still going up - more and more rocks and boulders, more of a steep incline. From there we could see the 'golden stairs' and it looks just like a rock slide. The ranger assured us it is much more difficult to climb in the summer as in the winter the snow is so deep they just carve out a staircase, hence the name the 'golden stairs'. Then it's just a matter of stepping up. Climbing up the stairs was often referred to as the "Chilkoot Step" and there is a famous picture of men ascending this stairway in the winter. The line is so tightly packed, that each man must keep on moving. If one tires or needs to rest, he must step aside and not impede the steady tramping of feet going up and up. But it still took the stampeders four and a half hours. Now you can see the orange wands sticking up between the boulders and put there by the rangers to mark the easiest route to the top. To the left of these wands, the boulders are smaller and loose. To the right they are large and steady. For the most part we tried to stay left, as I for sure could not reach over some of the larger boulders. But on the right, loose rocks was a big problem. It became a simple matter of clawing up on all fours, dragging my hiking stick behind me. Halfway up I was terrified to stand up, it was so incredibly steep that it seemed the weight of my backpack alone would make me tilt backwards and down over the boulders to the bottom, you would be cut to pieces on the jagged rocks. Occasionally there was a gap in the rocks and you looked down a hole that appeared bottomless. Other times you could hear water running far below. At first I tried making it from wand to wand but closer to the top it became one boulder at a time. I could never do that climb in the rain or snow, or worse, fog. It's a living graveyard. When we finally reached the top, our hearts sank to our boots to find a crater of boulders and another summit. A Ranger past us going down and nonchalantly advised us the mountain had false summits. It had precisely three summits and at each one we thought it was the last, but then another crater and another summit. Each crater had snow fields and here again was an ever present danger of walking off the mountain top for it was possible to walk too close to an edge that might collapse. Finally, at summit three we saw the Canadian Flag flying from a tiny warm-up shelter. Unless you have endured the misery, it's hard to comprehend the joy and overwhelming feeling of relief that we felt when we saw that flag. It was now 5.00 p.m. and we hurried to the cabin for our customary welcome to Canada, a cup of hot tea and certificate to authenticate our achievement. But to our absolute despair, there was nothing. The Ranger had left for the day and not a sole to be seen on this desolate windy summit. BJ by now was utterly exhausted and wanted to stop and make supper. But I was adamant I would not. On every wall of the shelter were signs, "DO NOT LINGER." We had already been told this the night before. The weather change up here is awesome and unpredictable and also, the creeks and rivers beyond swelled in the afternoon from snow melt and some could become unpassable. It was emphasized; one should get off the mountain as soon as possible. So, hungry and weary, off we set for Happy Camp, just five miles away. The longest five miles I have ever known. The landscape a vast tundra speckled with rocks, rocks and more rocks. They tore your boots, cut your hands and broke your finger nails. There was also the ever present threat of a twisted ankle as we lodged boots in between rock crevices. The distant horizon lay like a flat pencil line below the sky; there was nothing but rock and the occasional low vegetation. This goat path at times took us over thin ledges high above frozen lakes. At times the ledge would be so thin that only one boot would fit on it and to your left, a sheer drop down a granite face and a slide into a freezing glacier lake. At another time we crossed long scree, with no ledge at all and the loose rocks underfoot went trickling down into yet another lake. But this one was especially taunting, this lake had a solid ice cap, with some melting at the edges. Should you slip down with the scree into that lake its Good-Bye Charlie as under the ice cap you go and into the deep dark freezing cold water. You just put all your concentration on how and where you placed each foot. It seemed this walk to happy Camp would never end. The horizon never changed and on and on we tramped. Happy Camp was supposed to be nestled in a clump of trees, but the vast empty land showed not a single tree anywhere. It became dusk and we were not stopping at all, just tramping forward crossing waterfalls and creeks. They had risen now and often we were well over our ankles in water, even when we used the stepping stones. Finally BJ refused to walk another inch until we filtered water and stopped to drink. He was right of course, I was plain fixated on getting to camp and I could see us spending the night on the tundra. I know it was important to stop now, we were slowly dehydrating. It's a great danger to allow this to happen and I know this, bad decisions can come from this state and the body starts to shut down. I was concerned we would have to make camp on the tundra; we were completely worn out and every time we crossed a ridge we saw another one that had to be climbed over. I cursed the stampeders for being so stupid! All the time this crazy goat path, was rising and falling above lakes, going round passes but then suddenly we saw a man standing by a lake. BJ perked up quickly "We're here or that man's lost as well." To our unbelieving eyes, it was indeed Happy Camp and I realized why it was so named.

While BJ hurriedly set up camp, I quickly heated soup in the warm up cabin and then we were done for the day.

Safe in our tent, we tucked into our bags, the wind from the coast screamed and howled and yanked at the tent. BJ had to go out several times to secure the pegs. This is a wild and windswept lonely outpost.

Brigitte and Erik had just set up their tent, she said they only got there 15 minutes ahead of us and they too were bushed. The northern lights were on but only in white and we were too tired to watch them anyway. In the camp register next morning I read they had been "magnificent and colourful."

This morning we woke feeling a little more normal, we were packed and away by 10.30 a.m. The walking now is a little easier, but first, just for good measure, a huge ridge to climb up and over and back to the good old tundra then another ledge over a yawning canyon with a raging river racing along the bottom. We made a rest stop half way and made tea. A few other hikers were already there, the couple from the States, two American men and a young German lad on his own. Deep Lake was a lovely place to stop and rest, we bathed in the warm sun, not quite whole again, but getting along OK. From there a narrow ledge took us over another canyon, then into the woods (we are back in the land of trees). We arrived here at Lindeman at 3.00 p.m. to our mutual relief. We met Brigitte who is whacked and has sore legs; she went straight into her sleeping bag under a tree. While BJ set up our tent I cooked us oriental rice with sweet and sour sauce and made a large pot of coffee. BJ is running a fever and has no appetite, I'm hoping he is well enough to hike out tomorrow; it is a long day, about eight miles to Bennett Lake. I went to bed at 5.00 p.m. BJ is already in his sleeping bag, we both needed to rest and BJ must get rid of his fever.

Back at the Scales and Golden Stairs we saw lots of artefacts. Cable, horse bones, glass, ceramics, rusty tins, parts of wood stoves and here at Lindeman City the ground is strewn with nails, cans, (especially sardine) more horse bones, pots, pans and glass everywhere. Reading the history of this trail I'm horrified at the scope of animal cruelty that prevailed. It's easy to see why so many horses had broken legs, the constant climbing over all of those rocks, even human legs get wedged. I know mine did, more than once, no matter how gingerly I climbed.

It is now 9.00 p.m. and as I write, the wind is roaring outside, it's the first time I have slept without the sound of rushing water. Tonight though, the howling wind fills the void. Occasionally Erik and Brigitte's voice drifts over, but then just wind racing through this valley. BJ is asleep but he may have to get up and tie down some straps again. I am going to crawl down into my sleeping bag, my bones are sore and the ground feels hard.

Diane Campbell Thompson

Monday, September 1st, Bennett Lake: 9.30p.m.

Yesterday we left Lindeman City at about 9.00 a.m. under another sunny sky. Because of the bear problem, we have had to leave in groups, so we are hiking with Clara and Rupert which has made for a very pleasant day as we chatted almost the whole way. A sign at the trail head read "Caution, Bear on Trail." Apparently, two men, each hiking solo, were confronted by a bear. The first man dropped his pack and climbed a tree. He reported that the bear climbed the tree after him then went back down to get the pack. He bit into the water bottle and then climbed the tree again. After some minutes, the bear backed away and the man ran back to camp. A ranger went back to retrieve the backpack but couldn't find it. The man was so disoriented; he couldn't place exactly where he had been. The second man had the same experience, except he left his pack at the bottom of the tree. The bear again bit into the water bottle, but this time he tasted chocolate milk. It is because of this the bear is now considered a danger, since he now associates a backpack with chocolate milk. They have found a dead bear on the highway, fitting this bears description (don't they all look alike?) but since the rangers are only ninety per cent sure they have the real culprit, we all have to move ahead in groups. The place must be crawling with this top of the food chain animal; so many trees are covered in bear scratch. We are also with Brigitte and Erik and the ex-army guy and his companion. Of course, what would it be without a few ridges or so, but the last mile and a half saw us in sand as we crossed a miniature dessert. We come upon a mass of tree stumps where trees were felled to build boats for the last push to Dawson city via the rivers and lakes. A cemetery on a hill contained very crude wooden crosses or boards, people who died here at Bennett Lake. One states a man aged 62 years who left his wife and family in Quebec.

Again the ground is strewn with remnants of the struggle to reach the gold mines. Large bottle dumps showing they must have been heavy drinkers, rotting spam and sardine cans, a washing machine, mattress springs, remains of a rubber boot, a lady's boot with tiny buttons still intact.

There was a heavy yip yipping when we finally arrived at Bennett Lake, the blowing of whistles, hugs and congratulations and the exchanging of addresses by everyone. Brigitte has invited me to Key Largo to go sailing with her and Clara and Rupert have invited us to a weekend at their farm.

The Bennett Lake campground feels like a forsaken outpost. Its raw beauty is un-matched; the forbidding mountains that dip their feet deep into the glacier waters of the lake loom as silent watchmen. There is a well preserved train station and a large old wooden church. We are the only signs of life and our little tribe is huddled in the bosom of these mountains. Everyone is tired and burrow early into their tents. Silence descends as the moon and stars emerge. The wind hustles through this high valley, moaning from one end to the other. Someone begins to play a recorder, the notes drift dreamily through the air and the wind shushes and coos, the lake laps lazily on the sandy shore. I push deeper into my sleeping bag and staring at the gently flapping green walls of our tiny tent, lie spellbound.

In the early morning we are sitting in the train station waiting for the train to arrive; Brigitte is waiting for the ferry to go across Bennett Lake. The weather is cool, the wind is still with us and the sky is a Dresden blue canopy. The sand flies have coerced us all to take refuge in the station where we await the steam train to take us back to Skagway. After some three hours, the whistle of a steam train is heard and rushing outside en-masse, we see huge puffs of smoke billowing over the trees and soon a big black engine comes chugging into view. Hundreds of tourists on board are leaning out of windows snapping pictures

125

of the vagabonds loitering at the station, as we in turn were taking pictures of them. What a sight it was and because it was so overwhelmingly breath-taking, the train backed up for an encore performance. A film was being produced of this train journey to Bennett Lake and so encore acts would be repeated on the way back down, allowing us many opportunities to get off and take some great photographs. A special car has been designated for the smelly backpackers plus a separate open baggage cart for our packs. There is time for the tourists to check out the wooden church and stroll along the banks of Bennett Lake before we chug back down.

As I sit on the old steam train to descend to Skagway, I reflect on the past five days and feel as if I'm just waking from a dream. This historic trail will be etched in my mind for all eternity. The staggering and fearsome beauty of the coastal mountains, its lakes and valleys are something you must walk up to, to truly sense their magnificence. A car trip to this world is not possible; you must stand at the foot of this range and then enter into it. It is cathartic and I am so humbled to have been a part of it for a while.

I'm also happy I don't have to hike tomorrow, I burst my blisters last night and my feet feel soooo much better.

WW11 Anderson Shelter like the one we hid in.

My brother and I on Guy Fawkes day in our back garden at Humberston, note he wears one of our war time gask masks.

"Chad" as my father taught us to draw him

Sand dunes and beach at Humberston

Canoe trip to Cathedral Mountain on Atlin Lake

The Wardair plane at Junneau

Skagway Harbour with the Alaska Ferry in the foreground

Dead Horse Gulch, Alaska

Climbing the scales on the Chilkoot Trail

Whitehorse, with Smiley, a Quest runner

Crossing Annie Lake in the Yukon with
Cactus, Helix, Junior and Hooey

My Tipi home on Bear Island

My bed inside the Tipi, and fireplace in the foreground

Sailing in the British Virgin Islands

Me with my Grandmother Clarke

My grandmother and grandfather Anderson

My parents, taken at Humberston

Woodland wedding procession, Marcelline and Rachel foreground, Josee with Clara and Emma at the back.

Celebration on the Bruce Trail, back row from left to right:
daughter Marcelline, daughter in law, Josee, sister, Peggy,
Niece Kate: front row: grandchildren, Clara and Liam

Nick at the Boston Marathon 2005

Celebrating my 73rd birthday at Humberson, UK, with long time friends, Ron Fletcher and Carol Welldrake.

Richie's Hunt Camp in Nova Scotia

Miles Canyon, Yukon Territory

Skai and I rest on the road to Santiago

El Camino de Santiago 2013

YUKON QUEST 97

Flying north to the Yukon in February may seem counter intuitive, especially when the whole world it seems is heading for the sunny south. But if you want to witness the world's toughest dog sled race and some truly amazing dogs, then this is the destination for you. And while you are there, fall under *"The Spell of the Yukon"* as promised by Robert Service.

The Yukon Quest International Dog Sled Race takes place every February. A maximum of fifty mushers harness fourteen dog teams and head out on a 1000 mile (1600 km) run between Fairbanks Alaska and Whitehorse Yukon. In even years the dogs leave Fairbanks and in odd years they run out of Whitehorse. Heralded as the toughest race in the world, the Quest is the ultimate test of strength and mental stamina. There are seven checkpoints where mushers can stock up on supplies and food (compared to more than twenty in the "other" race in Alaska, known as the Iditarod). Quest teams must also cross three mountain summits, the Iditarod only one. Dog drivers cannot receive assistance other than the mandatory 36 hour lay-over in Dawson City.

It was a bleak and miserable February in Toronto when my spirits sagged to zero that I had a flash of inspiration. I will go to the Yukon and volunteer on the Quest. Where the idea came from I have no idea, only that in the dim recesses of my mind I had heard of the Quest and I am in love with the romance that is the Yukon. So, just as fools rush in where angels fear to tread, I naively phoned the Quest office in Whitehorse and asked if they wanted any help. The answer was simple….Yes! I needed no other command and before you could say "Mush" I was on a plane headed for the great white north. Here is part of my journal from that memorable adventure.

Tuesday, February 6th, 1997:

Left Toronto at 8.00 a.m. by limo. I wanted to indulge myself, with a large limo and a uniformed chauffeur, I settled for a large black car driven by a very polite man with a Punjab accent and a very neat turban. Breakfast at the airport was three dollars and forty eight cents for coffee and a muffin. We boarded at 9.45 a.m. and at first I thought I must be going to the Orient, mostly Chinese passengers, even Chinese hostesses and we got our message four times-in English; French; Chinese and Japanese. Lunch was chicken with rice, fruit salad and cake. Feeling slightly queasy I slept heavily after the meal. Interesting to fly over the Rockies, where I looked down on miles and miles of jagged mountain ranges, all snow topped and with lots of dark green firs on the sides and bottom. Those ridges look razor sharp and I wondered how wide they may be for walking along. Our arrival in Vancouver was 25 minutes early, plenty of time to eat a Mars Bar and drink a bottle of juice. I watched our plane for Whitehorse being prepped; it carries 100 passengers and is full. Lunch on this leg is the same as the previous, but this time I picked beef with rice followed by fruit and cake and a bite size Mars Bar!

An uneventful two hours with mostly cloud cover below, but we landed in Whitehorse at 3.00 p.m. to sunny skies and two degrees on the plus side. Taxi ride cost $11.85 and I was only in the car five minutes. My room at the High Country Inn is OK but not worth $79.00. I have a small kitchen and am situated on the ground floor overlooking a side street. I cached my breakfast food; bananas, oatmeal and snacks of pop and chips. I have a fridge also, so I'm hoping to save on food expenses.

After dumping my gear, I went for a walk to get my bearings. I always feel as if I have arrived home after a long absence when I go to Whitehorse.

Diane Campbell Thompson

Friday February 7th. 1997;

Sunny, minus 7 degrees

Left for the Quest office in the early morning dark at 8.30 a.m. and as luck would have it found Kathy Swenson's dog team tied up at the back of the hotel. About a dozen dogs sitting amongst bales of straw. Mostly Siberian huskies with piercing wolf like eyes. I stopped to snap some pictures when suddenly there was movement from the roof of the nearby pickup truck, it was the dog handler and he had slept there all night to watch over the dogs. We chatted for a while and he told me all of the dogs would be racing and pointed out the leader, a veteran of the trail. I asked him if I could have a picture taken with the pack and he was most happy to accommodate. Sitting with the dogs in a bed of straw, I was directed to sit next to "Smiley" who would literally smile for the camera and he did. (It was a great tragedy that one of these dogs would die on the trail and Kathy would withdraw from the race)

At the Quest office I met the manager and secretary who both instantly set me to work. With fellow volunteers, Charlotte from Prince Edward Sound in Alaska, Mike a snow maker from Northern Alberta; Bill from Scotland and Candice and Gregg from Banff, we set to work making media and vet tags. We all sat on the floor, shooting the breeze, making jokes and generally having lots of fun. Many mushers came in for blankets, doggy boots and first aid books etc. Everyone is extremely friendly and come in to say Hi as if they had known us forever. One handler brought in a pure black husky who had got caught in a dog fight and needed stitches. The poor thing seemed stressed and was shaking from head to toe. His name was Nome.

Charlotte and I left the office early and I have decided to check into her hotel "The Regina" who will give quest volunteers a room for $29.00, that's $50.00 per night cheaper than the High Country Inn. We spent the afternoon musing around the shops and ended at a photography studio where we each had our *pictures taken as mushers. We laughed hysterically as each posed on a sled with a team of stuffed huskies in a make believe world of snow and mountains, complete with a large whip that was a last minute prop provided by the proprietor.*

Tomorrow is a very early start as I'm being picked up after work for an afternoon of dog sledding by "Michie Mushers." I made some telephone calls yesterday to find out where I can try dog sledding myself and this looks to be a good place to try out. Charlotte has decided to join me; we will travel approximately one hour out of Whitehorse then sled for four hours. Dinner is to follow then a quiet evening in their guest cabin. After breakfast, we will be delivered back to Whitehorse for the start of the Quest at 8.30 a.m. I can hardly wait, I have been longing to try dog sledding and I will have my own team. Meanwhile, the weather in town is very mild and the mushers are concerned that the weather is too warm. They need minus twenty degrees and today was only minus six. The warm weather will make the going slow and will be harder on the dogs. They will actually have to truck in some snow to make the chute.

Must go to sleep now, I feel very tired and my flu bug is still around, right now I have a very sore throat.

Saturday, February 8th, 1997:

Temperature minus 16

Much colder today, the snow is crunching under my feet and my nose freezes as I walk to the Quest office. No one was there and Patrick was running a press conference so I went shopping. I wanted to get a coyote ruff but the Indian Store was closed. Back again at the Quest office I went to work counting out doggie booties for the drop-off points and sorted Media Accreditations and Releases. Chris from Michie Mushers picked up Charlotte and me at noon and after picking up three pizzas to eat on the way we set our sights on the ride out of town. It took us a good hour and then some to get back to their cabin in the bush. Michie Mushers sits on fifteen acres and shares the land with two other cabins, all out of sight of each other. As we arrived at our destination I was struck by a truly wondrous sight! – 22 dogs tied up in the bush - each with a kennel and pile of hay and all howling and barking. Chris wasted no time in teaching us the basics, how to ready the dogs and harness. He showed us how to take the dogs one by one, holding them up on their two hind legs, because on four they can run. Every dog there wanted to go and each one howled and yelped "Pick me, pick me." The din was enormous and we could hardly hear the next set of instructions....sled handling. There are three sets of brakes, a tire mat; spikes and a throw hook. As we start the business of harness fitting, the dogs go wild, jumping, yelping, barking – all wanting to go, such passion I have never seen. Chris said it is instinct, they just love to run, put a harness on a husky and he instinctively pulls, whereas you have to teach other dogs. He also warned us beforehand that once the harnessing started the dogs would go wild. We were also warned that once underway, the dogs will "go like hell" for about five miles before they settle down. And the warning was timely indeed neither was he talking to the breeze, that first pull was wild. Chris went first with six dogs, followed by me with four dogs, then Charlotte with four dogs. As soon as Chris pulled out of the driveway and I pulled out the throw hook, my team leapt into action and like a rocket we were launched, with Chris' wife Suzette yelling "keep the brakes on going out the drive." I did, but the dogs still left like Batman on steroids and in my panic I dropped the throw hook in the basket instead of looping it on the handle bars. Now my emergency brake is dis-abled! I thought I might die with my one piece of solid brake in the basket and extremely out of reach. We went all the way down the road and turned right (gee) along the shoulder of the highway but high above the road; a quick turn into a narrow trail through the trees, then out into the open again. A jeep driver on the road rushed out of his car to take our pictures as we sped the narrow ledge up a steep incline and disappeared from view. The trail is narrow and winding and very bumpy. I haven't quite got the corners down pat and I have to duck all the time for tree branches - sometimes the sled swipes the trees and that is quite another experience! The dogs are racing like hell as if we are on some lifesaving mission, but I watch Chris ahead and finally figure I can stand on the runners and tap the rubber tire mat with my heel to slow us down a bit. Suddenly we burst out of the woods and all sixteen paws land on the flat icy surface of frozen Annie Lake. Now I am on the set of Dr. Zivago, the sky is brilliant blue, not a cloud to be seen, the dogs have now settled down to a gentle canter, the sled glides easily, we are surrounded on all sides by high snow covered peaks. The moment is magical and I shall carry this memory for ever. The sun creeps onto the mountain tops, we are tiny figures tracing across a vast landscape of white, silence reigns but for the swish of the runners and the padding of paws. We must have looked impressive, three teams crossing a vast snow covered landscape with a backdrop of high white glistening mountains. There are no trees to dodge, no winding narrow path, just this amazing broad vista and I can afford to stand back on the runners, take a slow breath and let the dogs take me wherever.

The lake crossing took 45 minutes before again entering the bush. These trails are wider and lead us to a highway crossing and the next difficult section. This part of the trail is thick with trees, narrow and winding, bumpy, with some good climbs and drops. The experience becomes akin to flying downhill on a sled pulled by four crazed dogs..... and this is with both feet on the spikes. Forget the flimsy rubber mat this time. I have to admit I was panicking somewhat when the rear dog looked back at me over his shoulder and with a look that definitely said "get your foot off the *!*! brake lady," which I promptly did and apologized profusely. Next we cross a river and land onto another open plateau. Thank goodness for a rest stop! We have stopped here for hot tea and brownies and the dogs hungrily consume big chunks of frozen whitefish. I have my picture taken *with "my" dogs whose names are Cactus (my lead dog and veteran of the Quest) Helix; Junior and Hooey. After we have all re-organized ourselves, we get back on the sleds to do the whole trail in reverse, passing a team of fourteen on the way back. On the way Charlotte has fallen off twice and now has been moved behind Chris and in front of me. We have done this for two reasons, firstly so that Chris can catch the dogs as they sail past, as this was our first indication that something was wrong and secondly, looking back we saw Charlotte trudging along knee deep in snow. I can then pick her up as I sail pass. You see the dogs don't stop in their gay abandon and there is a slight technique to corners. It's a lot like skiing; you bend into the corners with your hips, not your shoulders as Charlotte was doing. I was able to master the corners easily, but alas, Charlotte toppled over at every bend as she leaned like the tower of Pisa and crashed.*

Once home, it's take off the harness's, clip dogs back onto their chains and put away all leads etc.

Suzette has cooked us a supper of Moose Lasagna, salad and huckleberry crumble with ice cream. The cabin is warm and spacious with a large wood stove in the middle of the wide open space. A bucket of water sits atop for hand washing etc. and we are seated at a long wooden table. After supper two pups are brought into the cabin for the night along with two dogs. Chris tells us that each night he rotates the dogs that come in to share the cabin.

There is another guest here also, Uvè from Germany. He is here to follow the Quest all the way to Fairbanks. Two years ago he travelled solo by canoe from Whitehorse to the Bering Sea, this journey took three months, now that is a true adventure.

Right now I am sitting in our cabin writing by lamplight. We have a large wood stove which Chris has stoked with fresh logs. We have a bucket of cold water on the small table plus a huge pot of hot water on the stove. There is no electricity or running water and the outhouse is close by with only a screen door, one does not linger there at this time of year despite the awesome

vista. Trooping out there before bedtime my flashlight is handy in the pitch black of the surrounding trees.
I have just cleaned my teeth, washed my face, I am going to turn out the lamp and sleep like a baby in this magical land.

Sunday; February 9*th*, 1997

Temperature minus 15

Up early and a quick trip to the outhouse at 6.35 a.m., it is dark and extremely cold, I hear footsteps outside the door and breathe a sigh of relief when I find it is only one of the dogs, my heart rate goes back to normal. Inside the main cabin we feast on pancakes and huckleberries, oranges and coffee. Uvè tells us of more of his adventures on the Cottonwood Trail in Kluane, solo of course and I am envious. It is beautiful he says and highly recommends it. But now we must all drive to Whitehorse in time for the volunteer meeting at 9.00 a.m. Chris and Suzette are working in the chute; this is where the dogs are fastened to the sleds and held before the take-off. I am told I can work with them to ready each dog. This is a serious quandary for me now, to be at the start and harness the dogs is a chance of a lifetime, but I also want to watch the start. I decide to watch and not work, but even so the decision is difficult. The whole of Whitehorse has assembled at the start and along the banks of the Yukon River. There are bleachers along the downtown start point which quickly fill. Media cameras and newsmen from all parts of Europe are here, plus the Mounties in full dress. I struggle too hard to catch everything on film, be it video or still or slide and run from point to point like a chicken without a head, spilling camera and film in the process. I catch the first three mushers as they leave then head further down the river for some excellent shots. The atmosphere is electric, the day crisp and clear, they have had to truck snow in to make the chute at the start point. The dogs are noisy and can be heard all over

159

town and down the river, everyone in a party mood, eating hot dogs and chili. Crowds cheer heartily as each musher leaves the chute and as I watch the dogs leap forward, I feel a lump in my throat at the enthusiasm, loyalty and bravery of both dogs and mushers as they leave on this epic crossing. What I would give to be on that ride. All too soon the last dog has left town and now it is uncomfortably quiet, almost unnatural, Charlotte and I had split up in the excitement, but find each other again in Tim Horton's, where we find Candice and Greg. Candice has an amazing Super Beaver Musher Hat and they both wear Steiger moccasin boots from Wisconsin. They purchased them mail order for 159.00 US$; not only do they look great but Greg tells us no other boots can compare. Now I want some.

Charlotte and I walk aimlessly around town, before going to eat supper at the Chinese Restaurant. Charlotte left for the airport and I walked around the deserted town once more before going back to the hotel. I met Bill from Scotland who has landed a job as handler and was heading to Fairbanks in a pickup truck.

I have just packed my bags and am about to take a long hot soak in the tub when the phone rings. It is Charlotte, "I can't get home" she says. Seems that Juneau, her destination, is all fogged in and she cannot leave. She has booked another room and I am waiting for her now. We are going down to the bar for some local entertainment, for a rye and ginger and some good conversation. We will reminisce about our week and then sadly it will be time to leave this town and this land which feels more like home to me every time I come here.

Back home again I follow the Quest in the newspaper and am filled with grief as I hear that one of Kathy Swenson's dogs has died. Kathy has withdrawn from the race. The dogs are highly respected and it is a serious blow to a musher to lose a dog. As the badge on my backpack proudly states "You've gotta love these dogs."

"They say God was tired when he made it

They say it's a fine land to shun

Maybe, but there's some who would trade it

For no land on earth..... and I'm one.   Robert Service:
The Spell of the Yukon"

Pleasures of the Sled Dog Trail

What fun and provocation are mixed in driving a dog sled team! Some of the dogs bark and almost knock one down in their anxiety to get the harness on. They start off at a full gallop on a good piece of trail, barking and tail wagging, making you puff to keep up. They get ahead, find a bad place, get stuck and Jack the 'wheel dog' who can do almost anything but talk, slips out of his harness. He takes a few rolls in the snow for refreshment and comes yelping back to meet us. If the others do not pull when starting, Jack barks at them, as if ashamed that they do not make their bodies swell behind the collars, as he does.

But how quickly they can make one's feelings change. Attracted by some side issue, the leader bolts from the trail. In spite of 'haws and gees' roared by the driver, in spite of frantic pulls on the 'guide-rope' attached to the sled, away we go, sled and load dogs and driver, in one bundle of fifteen feet down the embankment! And then the fuss begins. As you pick yourself up, recover your bearings and dig the snow out of your eyes, the dogs are busily engaged in weaving the harness into a braid of complicated patterns. You right your sled (that's all, for its load must always be lashed before starting so as to need no reloading) and start to undo the braiding. You get Nell, the 'leader' straightened out, hitch her traces into those of Ginger and his-if you can keep him still long enough-into those of Flora.

But while you are hitching Flora to Jack and Jack to the sled, Ginger has rolled over fifteen times as a past time! You don't unhitch Ginger again, for you're tired with snaps. While you roll him back fifteen times to get the kinks out of the tugs (and out of your own temper) Jack gets cold, slips the harness, which he can always do in a second and you feel his cold nose poked in your face, seemingly asking, "When are you likely to be ready to start?" But Jack is quickly forgiven, for as you lift his harness he is into the collar again in a flash.

You get started again. Soon you meet another dog-team, containing a scrapping dog. He snarls a challenge at Ginger as he passes. Ginger, always on the lookout for a diversion, answers with a lightning spring at this throat. In an instant, not two, but ten dogs are locked in a rough and tumble tumult. The 'harness braiding' goes on again, the pattern this time more elaborate and more complicated, for now it involves twice as many straps, with legs and tails, patches of detached hair and stripes of red blood thrown in for heightened effect. Lucky you are if the drivers do not catch the fire and add a few oaths and blows directed at one another.

From Mission: Klondike
James A Sinclair

Written for the Sunday school paper the Presbyterian "Kings Own" 1900

THE BRUCE TRAIL

With approximately 800 km (500m) of main trail and 200 km (125m) of side trails, the Bruce Trail is the oldest and longest marked hiking trail in Canada. Starting from its southern terminus at Queenston near Niagara Falls, the trail follows the edge of the Niagara Escarpment, a UNESCO World Biosphere Reserve. This well-marked trail passes through many diverse landscapes: wine fields in southern Ontario, major towns such as St. Catherines, Hamilton and Burlington, the Blue Mountains, Beaver Valley and finally the white cliffs of Georgian Bay. The main trail is divided into nine sections: *Niagara, Iroquoia, Toronto, Caledon, Dufferin Hi-Land, Blue Mountains, Beaver Valley, Sydenham* and *Peninsula*. Each section has its own subsidiary club and is responsible for local trail maintenance. White blazes, approximately 3 cm (1 in) wide and 8 cm (3 in) high mark the main trail, similar blue markers point to side trails. The trails' northern terminus in Tobermory is a jumping off point for Five Fathom National Park.

Rich in diversity, each section of the trail is unique in character. Teaming waterfalls, deep mossy glades, century old coniferous trees and towering Dolomite cliffs are just some of the natural wonders to be found. Rugged and remote the peninsula section is considered the *"jewel of the Bruce."* Starting in Wiarton, this section follows the shores of Georgian Bay with spectacular views of the deep blue waters of the bay. Hikes here can be challenging and steep with walks along narrow cliff ledges. A habitat for a variety of plants and mammals, the peninsula is also home to Ontario's only venomous snake the massassaga rattler. A stone cairn marking the trails' northern terminus sits by the picturesque bay of Tobermory.

By some lucky twist of fate, I met some people, sixteen to be exact and became part of this happy band, to walk the Bruce Trail from Niagara to Tobermory over a two year period.

Here are some random journal entries from that adventure:-

3rd line to Centre Road/89; November 3rd, 2001

Today, 26 of us left the start point at km 80.7 of map 19 under an overcast sky. While the temperature was cool (about 8°) it was perfect for a trek through the hillside. We had some strong winds but NO RAIN!

A good portion of the trail today was along fields in the rolling hills of the Dufferin Highlands.

All around us winter is creeping in, but each season brings its own special beauty. The palette is muted and pale. And while last week we were walking on a carpet of brilliant yellow leaves, this week our 'outdoor carpet' has turned a subtle shade of brown. The woods now are gray and the trees completely bare. Long grasses in the fields have turned the colour of straw. There is a strong smell of cedar and our brown carpet of leaves is soft underfoot. Milkweed pods are turned to grey with white down popping out. Some look as if they have been sprinkled with icing sugar.

Cynthia, who was one of the half dozen that has joined us for the day led us up a side trail in Mono Cliffs Park. This turned out to be a very interesting aside with the huge rocks of the escarpment towering high to each side of a narrow boardwalk. There are caves in this area and lots of green velvet moss clinging to the walls. We climbed down into a narrow opening in the rocks by means of an iron staircase. There is a lookout platform at the top of these stairs and we stood and waved to a large group of hikers below as they tramped the shores of a pond. This was our stop for elevenses.

Some confusion ensued when walking out of the park and Gord, sprightly scaling a wooden style to the right, was told he was going in the wrong direction. Advance hikers going straight ahead however had come to a dead end. Much discussion followed and a great many maps came out, brows furrowed with deep concentration. Peter finally solved the problem by showing that some kind soul had simply turned the sign post around. Gord had been right all the time, but this time he chose to hop the style, same as the masses.

Gord has also become our resident "stickman" having generously donated his time to standing by each wooden style we encounter and holding our hiking sticks as we climb over. I think it was more of a self-preservation move than a charitable donation when he saw me get "clobbered" on the head by a killer hiker who shall remain nameless!

The hike was completed by 2.20 p.m. and we headed to beer and coffee at the Bavarian House Tavern and nearby Coffee Time Donuts on Airport Road at Highway 89. The group then all departed for a convivial evening at the Mansfield Centre, or more affectionately christened "stalag 13" by Phil.

Tomorrow is hike number 24, 15km approximately to Dufferin Road 17.

Loree to Metcalfe Rock. May 11th, 2002; 18.8km

Another punctual start at 9.25 a.m. along green pastures complete with brown cows grazing. Our path today is best described as undulating-meaning what goes down must go up! The trail is proliferous with white trilliums; nodding lily white faces at the sun, not so the shy red ones, who blushingly hide behind shiny green leaves. The forest is bursting with spring and it seems can no longer contain its joy. We are surrounded by music, the brooks babble, robins, chickadees and blackbirds sing and Anne calls out "walking fern!" which her eagle eye has espied on a huge boulder. We are becoming amateur botanists. Al is very sick today but he soldiers on, looking gaunt and pale. The sky is a calm aquamarine blue and not a cloud in sight. It is supposed to be only 10° but feels much warmer and my sweat band is working overtime. Since it is such a glorious day and because we have made such good time, we have decided to go a further 5km to Metcalfe Rock. What a treat we find here in the form of a rope climb that took us a full hour to navigate. Ropes were used to slide down into a rocky chasm, then all kinds of scrambling down there to get up and over again. Huge rock faces go down and Paul helped by giving us hand and foot holds. There were patches of the winter's snow down there, deep in the many crevasses.

Altogether a very satisfying escapade that took me out of my sleepy haze and quite woke me up from my trance-like stupor.

Crane Lake to Emmett Lake Road; Sunday October 20th, 2002; 16.1 km

Started out from the logging road at approximately 9.30a.m. Again quite a lot of road work, about 7km of it to Halfway Dump. The weather is cold and damp, with rain and hail added for interest. My hands became very cold over lunch, where we sat under the trees and slowly got soaked and colder. From lunch on it was pure HELL! Boulders and rocks made wet and slippery in the driving rain and hail. I fell three times and was christened "pinball." Several fell also, Leone, Mary Beth and Gord. We are not sure about Phil as he may have fallen but won't admit it. Gord has admitted to his, but since no witnesses can confirm it, it doesn't count. Wayne has also fallen. We finished around 3.30 p.m. and were glad to get back to the cars. Some great lookouts but we could not fully enjoy them in this foul weather.

A SHORT HIKE

All around me summer is fading too quickly. The flower boxes of bright pink busy Lizzies and blue lobelias are becoming a tangled mess of brown drooping stems. Sad to see! It occurs to me that the "white throat" has not called lately and so I suspect he has left the neighbourhood for sunnier climes. I have seen great gangs of birds swooping and flitting on to the telephone wires. An avian airport, assembled birds, waiting for clearance to fly south.

Today though, I am taking visitors on a short hike. It seems an age since I hit the trail and Sergei and Katia are from New York City, they are anxious to find "fresh air." We pile into my car and head for the cliffs to see the hawks. Up and up the cars noses over the gravelly road, shuddering and shaking on the shale. At the top is our reward. There is one hawk, he swoops and glides around us and we watch him as he plays among the thermals. Far down below us the cars amble along the main street and in the distance we can hear the hum of a tractor over on the golf course. Nestled in a small valley, our town seems to echo with an eerie silence now that the cottagers have all gone.

Turning our back on the hawk we take to the woods. I haven't been on this trail since the spring and I'm struck by the amount of deadfall. It seems everywhere you look a tree has toppled and is lying prostrate on the forest floor. We step over branches and tree trunks, but our path is good and well-marked. Sergio it appears is an authority on mushrooms and we see many. He tells us which trees we should look under. I have always been fascinated by mushrooms but I am by no means a scholar. Now that it's brought to our attention, the three of us start eagerly searching them out. We find them in abundance. Small white iridescent ones, orange curly ones, some frilled with lace or plain flat brown ones. Aha! Sergei has found a gem! Gently easing a long stemmed mushroom from the dark brown earth, he nurses it as if it might have been some major archeological find. "I will cook" he beams shyly in his strong Russian accent.

Katia and I walk over to examine this "flower of the forest." He cradles it in his hand and it smells of the earth, rich, fertile, organic. It will be delicious. We examine the smooth brown "roof" and the long white juicy stem smelling of sweet decay. Carefully it is slipped into a brown paper bag which Sergei has pulled from his pack. We find two more and my guests proudly carry their treasure back to the car.

Driving home at the end of the day, Katia closes her eyes; her head falls back in tired contentment. Sergei sitting at my side, alert, attentive, clutches his small brown bag, his dark eyes focused intently on the open road ahead; a secret smile walks across his face. I wonder what he is thinking.

EL CAMINO DE SANTIAGO

The Camino has been a siren call ever since reading Shirley Maclean's 2001 book on this ancient path. It was the thought that such a trail existed that attracted me. Up until then I had never entertained the idea of pilgrimage, although I have always enjoyed the long trail. Over the years, someone would mention the Camino, or I would meet someone who had done it or was about to do it. The recent movie *The Way* prodded me again to think of the Camino. It seemed that the Camino was calling me and there came a point I could no longer ignore it. This is my journal then of that long trail, which has proved to be not only rewarding in the physical sense but also a trail of soul stirring introspection and a new self-awareness.

Diane Campbell Thompson

Day 1: St Jean Pied de Porte

Wednesday, August 21st. Auberge de Pelerin (Priv)

I slept like a baby last night. The hostel in Paris was spacious, very new and spotlessly clean. We were up at 5.30 a.m. and away by 6.00 a.m. An easy single ride on the metro brought us effortlessly to the train station. We quickly found our platform despite the enormity of the place and even had time to pick up a café au lait and one of those fabulous fresh French croissants. The train, an ultra-modern high speed affair, had comfy ergonomic seats and lots of leg room. We pulled slowly out of the station and as the super train picked up speed I felt a flutter of excitement at the prospect of what lies ahead. I breathed a small sigh that at least we had come this far without upset and sat back to view the pastoral landscape of quaint stone cottages with umbra shutters and fields of bright yellow sunflowers that floated by our window.

At Bayonne we had a two hour wait for our connection and here we saw the first of many pilgrims. We talked with Jacquelyn from Quebec and a lady from Idaho who is meeting her husband here to hike the Camino together. The train to St. Jean, despite looking like a single speeding bullet, was one of the slowest I have ever travelled on. It must have been more a problem of track logistics I reckon. It was full to the hilt however with backpackers, cyclists and bicycles. A good six stops before St. Jean we began to see mountains, at first just gentle kindly looking ones. But on arriving in St. Jean we see the full catastrophe, the mighty Pyrenees looked forbidding but at the same time awesome with their battlements of green slopes. Skai excitedly took endless pictures through the train window and beamed in wide-eyed disbelief at the stunning vista.

At St. Jean Pied de Porte of course, in 31 degree heat and blazing afternoon sun, we lost our way walking into town. Gasping and breathing hard we dragged ourselves and packs like two old mules, in an out of streets before ending back at the train station. This was slaughter before we even put a foot on the Camino and I was seriously fagged out. I opted to drop the pack and walk all the way to the top of the town to find our Albergue and the Acquiel (Camino office). Having done that I then walked all the way down again, picked up my pack and told Skai we have to climb to the top of the hill as I had found the Albergue there; by now I was extremely flushed and feeling totally finished. As we started to climb the steep cobblestone street, Skai stopped abruptly, thinking she had found the Acquiel, (it was a souvenir shop selling shells). As Skai browsed the many shells on display, I continued to drag myself doggedly back up the steep hill. To my utter dismay, Skai stayed put, insisting this was where we needed to be and I despaired of ever having to go back down. But just then an Angel of Mercy appeared in the form of a Basque lady, who saved me from passing out with heatstroke, frustration and a bad case of temper. She called persistently "Madame" "Madame" and turning slowly I saw the lady pointing to me and then at the door she was sitting beside. It was the Acquiel and I was standing at it. Relieved I did not have to climb further I yelled down to Skai again, who was still down the hill browsing, still convinced that she had found the office and was now happily selecting a shell. My shouts down to her were totally in vain, she was lost in another world. I despaired again of having to go back down, when my dear Basque lady ran down and tapped her on the shoulder. Oh! Joy! Thanks for the kindness of a stranger, my dear Basque lady and my first Angel of the Camino, of whom I took a picture and shall be forever grateful to.

St Jean itself is a picture book town of steep cobblestone streets, terraced houses and abundant flowers in pots and on balconies. The name St. Jean Pied de Porte translates into English as Saint John at the foot of the mountain pass. *After registering in the Pilgrim office and getting our shells plus last minute trail updates, we checked into Auberge de Pelerin, conveniently next door to the Acquiel, which was not at the top of the street as I had mistakenly thought. Again, we have spotlessly clean accommodation, right on the main street. There is a small terrace at the back where we have dinner with five Frenchmen. Our room has four bunk beds and we are a total of six girls (I use this word loosely, as Skai and I are pushing 70 and 73 respectively, while the others are twenty something). Sabena from Germany; Astrid from Paris, Stella and friend from England, plus Skai and I. Dinner was one of the tastiest ever. A soup of pureed chick peas and onion (with garlic and lots of delicious herb combinations); Roast Duck legs, Beans with sage, Carrots in all kinds of herbs, scrumptious crispy roast potatoes, followed by a creamy caramel pudding and a small biscuit. All of this washed down with a bottle of rosé wine. If this be pilgrim fare, today we are two happy pilgrims.*

We made vain attempts at conversation with the Frenchmen, but their English was about as good as our French, so it was a bit stinted, but we did get across names etc. Two of the men were on a serious hike, having started to walk just south of Paris. They said there is a well-marked trail which goes all the way to Santiago.

After dinner we strolled up and down the busy cobblestone main street and I bought a pair of light weight shorts that fit perfectly and are drip dry.

Day 2: Orrison

Thursday, August 22nd, 2013

Refugio Orrison,	*distance*	*Ascent; 800m*
(priv. 18 beds)	*walked; 8km.*	

I slept well last night until three in the morning, when I lie awake listening to the church bell chime every thirty minutes until it was time to get up at 5.30 a.m. Breakfast was delicious, with fresh baguette, butter, jam, raisin cake, orange juice and coffee. Several pilgrims were seated at the table and there was a general hustle of comings and goings. At 7.00 a.m. we were out the door and in the dark. The climb is said to be extreme and since we didn't want to wear ourselves out the first day, we sent our packs ahead to Orrison.

The path was consistently steep, never letting up at all, but we stopped frequently as did the many others on the trail and overall found it manageable, especially since we were only going a total of 8km. My T-shirt quickly became soaked with sweat so I took it off and hiked with just my sports bra. We had brought sandwiches for lunch and decided we would stop at 11.00 a.m. anticipating our arrival at Orrison to be around 1.00 p.m. Imagine our shock and surprise, when we rounded a bend at 10.45 a.m. and walked smack into the Orrison Refugio. I couldn't believe it, only three and three quarter hours. I was sure we could only do 2km an hour on the climb, but we had managed more and feeling really OK at that.

We went straight in to get a fresh squeezed orange juice and sit at the terrace on the mountainside. Jacquelyn is here, also the man from Texas who is struggling very hard, he is overweight and has had to stop constantly. But he is determined to press on to Roncesvalles and we watch him as he leaves and wonder how he will make out. By 2.00 p.m. we have checked into our rooms, had a shower, done our laundry and hung it out to dry on the line at the back. Many pilgrims are here, as the restaurant

has beer, fresh squeezed orange juice and a full lunch menu. The Refugio is full, so pilgrims now have no choice but to carry on for another 19km. There is nothing between here and Roncesvalles, only the odd water fountain.
Dinner is at 6.30 p.m. and we are served a pilgrim meal of home-made minestrone soup, again with lots of fresh herbs; Roast Pork, Baked White Beans in a cream sauce, again enriched with herbs and pepper, followed by Chocolate Basque Cake. Of course, the usual bottle of wine, this time a red. I love the way they use herbs as opposed to spice, which I find hard to digest. Note to self, learn to cook with herbs.
We are 36 pilgrims for dinner and we sit across from Joanne and Jan from England, Doug from Moncton, New Brunswick, Canada, Shirley from England (who is walking for Harrys Heroes) and a youthful Lucas from Denmark. After dinner, we are asked to stand up in turn and introduce ourselves and say why we are walking the Camino.

Day 3: Roncesvalles

Friday, 23rd August, 2013

Monastery,   distance walked; 19km,   Ascent 650m
(183 beds)

*A tough day of climbing that took 9hr.15mins with few rest stops.
How come we were assured this day would be easier than the
last? It most definitely was not and I felt sorry for all those who
did not stay at Orisson because of this misinformation. Steep
climbs, interspersed with some small level patches where you
could catch your breath and stop your heart from jumping clean
out of your chest on a trail that seemed to have no end to it. On
the mountain, a black and white pony appeared out of the mist
and literally headed straight to me. It was magical and he stood
next to me for so long I was able to stroke his mane. We walked
part of the way with Kathryn from Ireland, then José from Spain.
Jose walked with us for quite a while and shared his tin tuna
with us, I traded him my small water bottle which I find useless
and José thinks it is great. Joanne and Doug caught up with
us briefly, (Jan has gone by taxi as she was violently vomiting
all night), but mostly we are alone since we are slow. My gouty
left toe joint is in agony, as is my left knee, despite wearing my
knee brace all day. We left in a light drizzle and a heavy mist
so thick we couldn't see beyond 50' in any direction. We had a
very long and steep descent into Roncesvalles stumbling in from
a woodland trail that went on so long I was convinced we were
lost. It ended at a quiet lonely T-junction with no indication of
which way to turn. Three Spanish girls caught up to us and we
all pondered which way to turn. The heavy mist had returned
and it was 5.00 p.m., I had serious thoughts about going back
up through the woods to see if we had missed a marker, but after
a short conference we all turned to the right. Just five minutes
later, there appeared the enormous shape of the Roncesvalles
convent, looming ghostly and tall through the mist. One of the*

177

girls behind us promptly fell to her knees and kissed the ground. It was like seeing a vision, eerie, but heaven-sent, what a relief it was. Once inside the huge building it was a hive of bodies, packs and boots. There are beds for 183 pilgrims and we each received a warm welcoming hug by the volunteer hosts there. We were directed to a room on the left, where boots had to be taken off and put on one of the rows and rows of shelves. It was like a library room, except the shelves were stacked with boots not books. The inside is extremely clean and new looking, there are three floors and we are on the second floor. A row of cubicles runs along the right side of an enormously long hall and each cubicle has two bunk beds with adjoining wooden cupboards. Two of the Spanish girls are sharing our cubicle, they are Ester and Vicki. After the usual shower and laundry, we go out to the restaurant for a pilgrim meal. The restaurant is pub style and packed. There is a line-up for dinner and we end up at a table with Jacquelyn and a new face, Sherri from Seattle. Our meal is again great, Soup, poached whole trout, French fries, Yogurt and the customary bottle of red wine. After dinner the four of us went to the Pilgrim mass in the cathedral, a beautiful service in which the countries of each pilgrim is called out. We are then called up to the Alter for a pilgrim blessing. I didn't understand much of the service, words not in Spanish were in Latin and I don't speak either. But it was nonetheless quite moving and uplifting.

As I write this now, I am snug in my upper berth; everyone here is super tired, as I am too, but it was, despite everything, a great day and I feel as if I have achieved greatness by walking over the Pyrenees.

Irish Kathryn told us later that when she had left us on the Pyrenees to walk ahead, she was determinedly walking, head down in the mist, when a car stopped and asked if she was OK. "Yes thanks" she said

"No you're not" said the driver, "you're going the wrong way" It appears she had wondered way off the trail and was walking into the wild blue yonder and, in a very heavy mist. The driver

took her back to where the Camino leaves the road and follows a grass track. Another Pilgrim was in the back seat, also picked up as having gone astray. There is the odd car along that remote road, they are, we are told, shepherds who are checking their flocks of sheep.We call them 'Shepard's in Citroens'. I don't think Kathryn was the first to go astray and the locals must have a lot of fun picking up the wanderers. Up in the Pyrenees though, that kind of mistake has cost lives.

Day 4: Zubiri

Saturday, 24th August, 2013

Municipal Refugio   distance walked   ascent 950m
Escuela, (52 beds)   21.9km

Another very tiring and long day with steep climbs and descents. We left in total darkness again and with more misty rain. After thirty minutes we were in Burgette and had breakfast of café con leche and a fresh croissant with cheese and tomato. As we walked out of the small town, an old man insisted on greeting us with a kiss on the cheek and having his picture taken with each of us.

From then on the climbing started again, up and down we go, the path is steep and rocky and oh so hard on the feet. The path led us through a witchcraft forest to Espinol then up to Alto Merquiriz at 950m, which of course then went extremely down to the village of Viskaret, where we had another café con leche. Onward and upward again on a rocky path to Alto de Erro. We met Joanne and Jan and were surprised to see Joanne as she had eaten nothing at all today. She has been throwing up and seems to have caught the same bug that Jan had yesterday. A truck parked by the roadside was a Godsend. We sat at the plastic tables and I bought a fresh apple, while Skai ate a banana. Ester and Vicki caught up to us here also, we are now like lost family when we meet, lots of hugs and happy to see a familiar face. Even Ester and Vicki, who are much younger than us, are weary and not thrilled at having to go another 3.6km to Zubiri. The soles of my feet are so sore, my knee also and last night I couldn't sleep for the pain in both hips when I lay down. Vicki and Ester say a Spanish recipe for sore muscles is sugar water, so at bedtime, along with my extra strength Ibuprofen, I also made up some sugar water.

This municipal Refugio sleeps 52, our room has seven bunk beds and we are eight as I write this now. We arrived at 5.00 p.m. and were the first in, so I quickly seized the shower. I did laundry also; washing two pair of socks, one bra, one T-shirt, one bandana and one pair of pants. I have hung them all out to dry, but there's little hope so I now have them decorating the rails of my bed. Feeling very tired and weary tonight and still having trouble trying to remember where things are in my pack, don't seem to have found a system yet. We have seen Jacquelyn here, also José, the latter we are trying to avoid. We are careful not to make eye contact with him, he talks so much and is so loud, plus he is hard to get rid of.

Pilgrim meal was excellent, mixed salad; steak and French fries, Custard, but no wine for me.

I think my pack is not adjusted properly, that is why my shoulders hurt so much. We hope to make Pamplona tomorrow and if it is not too hilly it is possible.

Day 5: Trinidad de Arres

Sunday, 25th August 2013

Albergue Hermanos Maristas Convent (41 beds)	distance walked; 16.4km	Ascent: 360m

I found the going very tough again today and am feeling extremely tired. My feet are sore; my shoulder muscles are killing me. At this point in time I am not looking forward to the days ahead with any great joy. I just want to go home and regretfully seem to have adopted a jaded outlook, comparing everything to Italy: of course Spain just does not measure up! I am hoping my outlook will change; I'm not usually so turned off when I travel.

Skai on the other hand is fairing much better, she seems totally unfazed and enthusiastically taking lots of pictures, talking cheerfully to everyone she meets. It's hardly surprising, she is in much better physical shape and she is jauntily striding along. I'm glad one of us is having a good time!

The trail today is almost all gravel path, many steep ups and downs again. I find this especially hard and just wish the day to be over. There were some pretty stretches along the Arga River; we walked through several small hamlets but no sign of life except for a few stray cats and one stray dog. But it is Sunday after all, when everything closes and life comes to a standstill. We fell into the first Albergue we came across, falling short of our goal at Pamplona by 5km. But this place is lovely, very old and has been accommodating pilgrims since the 11th century. Two large wooden doors marked the entrance and we had to ring a large doorbell to get in. A very kindly elderly man let us in, stamped our passports and invited us to the pilgrim mass tonight. Just as he was about to show us to our room, the doorbell rang and he scurried out to let three cyclists in. He led us all to the dorm through stone wall corridors and up ancient stone steps. There are nine bunks in our room and we both quickly snaffled a lower berth. As we were setting out our sleeping bags, we met Kathryn from Ireland again. Once more lots of joy and hugging as yet another family member re-appears.

We are slowly getting into the routine of things now and head directly to the shower, then to the sinks to do laundry. We hung everything outside on the line and sat in the garden to update our journals, also to read up on tomorrows hike. Oh my God! More mountains for heavens sake! It is quite cool now and we are off to find a restaurant for our pilgrim meal. The front door bell is ringing again, more pilgrims, or someone who just wants to come back in. The door is locked all the time and you can't get in at all after 9.30p.m.

Dinner was just OK, a really good salad to start, then not so great chicken and French fries followed by yogurt. I do not take the complimentary wine as I am on painkillers and I don't handle red wine too well anyway. Skai is something of a health scholar and always has red wine which she says is beneficial to her health as is lots of milk. Tonight she opted for rice pudding dessert, "I need to get some calcium into me" she chimed.

Back to the dorm and an early bed for me. My feet and shoulders are extremely painful so I took two ibuprofens today.

Tomorrow Pamplona, 5km.

Day 6: Zaraquigei

Monday, August 26th, 2013

Albergue Priv.   Distance Walked;   Ascent 250m
16 beds   16.4km.

The walk into Pamplona was simple and flat, through the suburbs then through ancient stone walls to the city centre. The huge medieval gate is impressive and has a huge and seemingly perfectly usable drawbridge. We found bank machines to replenish some euros and found time to sit in a restaurant for lunch. Everywhere, we see people (mostly men) walking home with huge fresh baguette's tucked under their arm. We have had a few sandwiches made from these and I can tell you they are teeth breakers. A Bocadillo (sandwich) is simply a baguette, cut in two then sliced down the middle. The filling can be anything you like, but mostly cheese or ham. They are super crusty, if you have false teeth, don't order one. The city itself is fascinating, a maze of narrow cobblestone streets and I can visualise the running of the bulls that takes place every year. We asked a man to show us which streets they actually ran down and stood to survey and try to imagine the chaos and the sound of hooves on cobbles. Leaving Pamplona we stopped at the university where they stamped our passports. The grounds were lovely and park like, so we decided to take a water break and to sit for a while on the grass, take off boots and socks and let our feet get some air. A good thing we did, for we had no idea what we were in for. Although only 3.6km the path up to the Zaraquigei was not only ridiculously rocky, but steep. The Albergue here is a privately owned one and is in a small mountain village. We decided to stay here as it was late afternoon and the alternative was to climb another 2.4km, then a steep descent to Uterga, where there are only two Refugio's, of which one is municipal. However, the reception here is in stark contrast to last night. First of all the hospitalera went into a frantic speech in Spanish to another woman there. The two seemed angry and asked if we had a reservation, which we did not. After much foreign dialogue we were finally accepted and told to go over to the computer and check ourselves in. The computer did not work and the hospitalera was determined not to help. Finally, we somehow got through it all and a line-up had grown behind us. This is actually a private home, with lovely furnishings downstairs and in the hall, but we are all shuffled upstairs. It is a disaster, the few rooms are full and only one bathroom is available with just two showers and a toilet. There is a second toilet downstairs. We share a room with a Basque family, two young girls, aged about ten and two older Basque women. It is a small bedroom, where the Basque group have a double size bunk; we have a single bunk pushed at a right angle to theirs. There is no room to walk between the beds, it is hot and stuffy. We learn that many other pilgrims have arrived and an Albergue that has accommodation for sixteen, now has forty bodies. They are everywhere, on couches, cramped in tiny rooms and now the line-up for the unisex shower and toilet is long. Since there is absolutely nowhere else to go we are all at the mercy of the vixen and her meagre staff. Everyone grumbles, everyone agrees the host is miserable. However, we are all accommodated at meal time and have a good meal despite our ills, but I cannot eat much, I am not feeling too good with a queasy stomach. Across from us sit a French couple, mid-thirties and looking very fit and athletic. With the help of food and wine, people relax and soon forget the petty complaints and enjoy good conversations. At bedtime, Skai lapses into a coma-like sleep and instantly starts to snore, very loudly. The Basque lady is not amused, she starts clicking her tongue at Skai, who stops for a second or two then resumes. The woman then starts saying shhh... shhhh.shhh, louder and louder. This doesn't work either, so I start hitting Skai's mattress.

We try in vain, but Skai is off in deep slumber and we can only wait wide eyed for dawn to break.

Diane Campbell Thompson

Day 7: Maneru

Tuesday, August 27th, 2013

| Albergue Lurgorri, | Distance walked | Ascent 820m |
| Priv. 12 beds | 17.6km. | |

Today we continued up and it is no easier first thing in the morning than late in the afternoon. An Australian girl who we met on the way up was trying a new approach on the climbs. It was this, you count to eight, with one through five, being counted steps and for six-seven and eight you stand still. Not only do you rest often, but you start each time on the opposite leg, so you don't wear out one side before the other! We tried this routine for a while and then gave up, no matter how you slice it; this is a bitch of a hill. Once up there, we were with the wind turbines and hundreds of them all along the ridge and stretching as far as the eye could see into the distance. All of them were moving well, but not as noisy as I had expected. The power company has erected a tribute to the pilgrims here in the form of a series of wrought iron images depicting pilgrims through the ages, all bent into the wind and looking towards Santiago. They stand at the foot of the windmills atop the high ridge in one long impressive work of art.

We lingered atop the cold and windy ridge to survey the panorama stretched out below us before taking the descent down which became something akin to a sheer drop and every bit as cobbled as going up.

A stop for breakfast in Uterga, saw me devour apple pie with my now usual café con leche, plus an apple to go for the trail. We also had to stop to doctor one of my toes; I had a blister two days before, not a big one at all, just a small one under the second toe. I did the needle and thread soaked in iodine routine and it worked, except the plaster I put on has slipped and is now causing friction between the toes, so I have replaced it with moleskin. I adjusted my pack and now my shoulders are not so sore, but my feet feel like someone has beaten the soles with a baseball bat. We also got lost coming out of Puente La Reina and ended walking on the highway for 4km, all uphill, in the searing heat. Grrrrrrrr, felt as if I had been sent to purgatory. Other than that it was a great day.

Pilgrims meal is at 7.00 p.m. tonight and I intend to go right to bed afterwards. I have not had a decent night sleep yet and last night put the cap on it. The dorm here is very nice and quite spacious. There are eight bunks, a very pleasant garden adjoins the room, the two showers are excellent and the hospitalero extremely pleasant. I am sitting in the garden as I write now, having done my laundry like a good pilgrim; it is hanging on the line, though I doubt it will dry. We never get anywhere before 4.00 p.m. which doesn't give wool socks much time to dry, especially when we only hand wring everything.

At dinner we are like the United Nations; South Korea, Italy, Australia, Ireland, Germany, France and Canada. Dinner prepared by our host is excellent; salad to start and I love these Spanish salads. It is the dressing for sure, but more than that, the presentation of it, such a piece of art, usually served on a large oval platter, with lots of fresh greens, shredded carrots, olives, white asparagus. Then another plate of sliced tomatoes, drizzled again with the oil/vinegar dressing and lots of fresh garlic grated on top. Next was a huge dish of Paella. The young Frenchman who was cycling had come from St. Jean Pied de Port that day! That's 105km and we have taken six days to get here. He hopes to do the entire Camino in one week.

One feels very quickly a part of this pilgrim fraternity, it's a strong family and we are kindred spirits. Everyone is so supportive and concerned for each other, always a Buen Camino. Even the Spanish greet us this way and on the street today a striking man softly uttered "Buen Chi Chico" as I passed him.

Day 8: Estella

Wednesday, 28th August, 2013

Pension San Martin   distance walked 21km.   Ascent 100m

"What temperature do you serve cheesecake at?"
We were walking under a cloudless sky through miles of golden wheat fields and I was drinking in the peace and tranquility of the trail. I tend to drift off in thought at times; hiking to me often becomes a walking meditation where I can do a lot of mental house-cleaning. Sometimes I recite a poem to myself, "The Spell of the Yukon" by Robert Service is my favourite, it's long and I memorized all nine verses while hiking the Bruce Trail, another favourite is "Riches I hold in light esteem" by Emily Bronte. But for some reason lately, I have been humming the 18th century ballad, "Do ye ken John Peel" to myself, it's become one of those tunes that keeps nagging over and over in your head and won't go away. So it was something of a shock to my senses when the voice crisply cut into my wistful state of mind.
Looking around in confusion, I turned to see Skai looking directly at me. I was momentarily bewildered and it took some time for me to re-focus.
"From the fridge or at room temperature?" she questioned.
I scrambled to focus my brain into active mode.
"Err, fridge, I guess."
"Well, you see that's wrong" was the quick reply, "It should be at room temperature."
Now I know I'm not a talker, I tend more towards the silent type, cocktail parties are a nightmare. Hopeless at small talk I suddenly realise that my silence may be making Skai uncomfortable. I simply cannot conjure up a conversation about nothing. I know many people can and I take my hat off to them, it can be a great ice-breaker. I am frequently amazed at some people's ability to make idle conversation. For instance,

I remember clearly being totally astounded as I listened to someone talk non-stop for twenty minutes about the qualities of a bakers rack. That is hugely clever. Other than saying it looks nice or not and what do you put on it, I'm pretty well done with the subject. Skai is a neighbour of mine, we have not spent a lot of time together and perhaps I do not know her as well as I thought or she me.

Walking with me may be challenging in this regard and I'm always happy to see someone temporarily catch up with us, for then Skai can dive right into conversation and I can relax and go back into myself. The question so startled me that I think I will never take cheesecake out of the fridge again without flinching. All this aside, today was comparatively easy and pleasant, after the climb to Ciraqui, a picturesque medieval hilltop city. Then the usual terrific downs followed by the usual climb back up to Lorca, where we had our first café con leche. We walked then into Villatuerta at 1.30 p.m. and were feeling fine so decided to march on to Estella. Again, a rocky path, intense heat and of course, a few more climbs for good measure saw us in Estella just one hour later. We are getting better at this. We entered the first bar we came to for fabulous fresh squeezed orange juice. The orange juice is always fresh squeezed; they have a remarkable machine that is constantly fed whole unpeeled oranges when an order is placed. They must go through boxes of oranges.

Feeling hot and bothered we started searching for an Albergue so went over to the tourist office. Closed! It is siesta, how silly of us not to remember. You'd think at least someone can man the information booth in the afternoon. We ended up wandering narrow cobble streets for over half an hour to find this little oasis in the desert. I can't tell you the joy to get off my feet. We have a delicious room, with SHEETS! TWIN BEDS! TOWELS! Hallelujah! This is costing 20€ each with no meals. It's perfectly acceptable to splurge once in a while and its doing wonders for my spirit. We have done our laundry again, showered and everything is perfect in the world of loaves and fishes. Skai, after a week of living sparsely, was confused at the abundance of towels I guess, because after we had showered, she said "Oh look, there's more towels." We each had one on our bed, I went ahead and used mine and hung it in the bathroom afterwards, Skai went into the bathroom, showered and used my wet towel again before noticing the unused one on her bed! Yuk.

Last night in the Albergue, the Korean man went over to the Irish lady and said he would change bunks with her. She had a top bunk and he had a bottom one, next to his wife on the far side of the room. The Irish lady was completely overwhelmed by his generosity and said she did find it hard to climb up and down. He carried all her stuff and pack across the room to his bunk.

Day 9: Los Arcos

Thursday, Casa de la Abuela; (priv) 30 beds;

Thursday, August 29, 2013.	distance walked 22.9km	Ascent; 370m

22.9km. from Montjardin to Los Arcos sheer murder. Flat, hot, hot and hot, with nary an inch of shade to be found anywhere. Literally fell into this Private Albergue for 35€ per night where we had reserved a private room – excellent!

We sent the packs ahead today and thank goodness we did, for as soon as it hits noon we cook. It was 9km of dusty trail over farmland; we go up to a village, we go down the other side. The last 9km was nothing more than an exercise in torture, searing heat, no shade, no water fountains, we march like robots. With every step my hips let me know passionately they are with me and tonight my feet feel as if I have just spent a week in Guantanamo Bay and have been flogged with a baseball bat. I just feel at times completely overcome and a bus ride to the end is what I really need and then all of a sudden something good comes along to revive the soul. As we walked into a hamlet, an old man standing in his garden beckoned us over. He gave us each a handful of juicy green plums from his orchard. Oh such divine heaven, our dry and parched mouths soaked up every drop of juicy sweetness which ran down our chins and through our fingers. Never did I taste such plums and I doubt I ever will again. My second angel of the Camino.

Having a private room is also such a lovely change. I would love to take a bus tomorrow to Logrono, but will deliberately march on to Viana. I dread it actually as my left foot is still sore from the blister I had a few days back. I did do the needle and thread operation with iodine and it worked well and this morning I had put antibiotic on it. But is still feeling raw, so I put a Doctor Scholl Blister pack on it which is supposed to stay on until it falls off.

I am just now sitting in the plaza waiting for supper, I find it chilly.

A young couple with a baby own this Albergue and they work like slaves all day and night with us band of strangers to cater to. The wife does laundry for 50cents, ridiculously cheap, so I have given her everything. I'm hoping everything will dry as I don't want to hike in these leggings, then I will seriously wilt in the heat tomorrow.

Today also was the day of the wine fountain (Fuente de Vino) at Irache, where courtesy of the Bodegas wine company, pilgrims can quench their thirst not only with water but red wine. In a tiny enclosed courtyard, on an impressive stainless steel panel on the stone wall, we have two spigots to pick from, marked "Vino" and "Agua." The custom is to take a sample of wine in your shell, which I did, but of course there is always someone who fills their water bottle. The fountain is right on the trail, impossible to miss.

Day 10: Viana

Albergue Izar. Priv

Friday, 30th	distance walked	Ascent 300m
August, 2013	20km	

Yet another day in purgatory! (Why did I decide to do this anyway?) None of the days so far have been easy; at least that is my experience. Although I am undoubtedly stronger, the steep climbs and harrowing descents are taxing to put it mildly. Even those young macho men on bikes with their fancy streamlined gear and helmets were puffing and gasping on the climbs and again we have searing heat with no place to hide in the shade. This is from the Brierley guide for this section 'This is a long stage and there are some short but very steep sections into the rio Linares (Torrres del Río) and Cornava river valley, so be particularly mindful when negotiating steep paths' believe me, he wasn't kidding. My blistered toe is slightly better, but still gives a little twinge right through the toe. Now the toe on my right foot is looking suspicious, so I have put some moleskin on it. I had put duct tape on but I had also covered my feet in Vaseline so it fell off. Today my left knee is angry, my back aches and the sole of my feet still hurt. I read somewhere that pilgrims are supposed to suffer. OK, I think I have done my bit and it's time someone cut me some slack.

On a brighter note, there was a lovely Knight Templar church (Iglesia de Santo Sepulcro) in Torres de Río where I paid 1€ to go inside. For me, it was well worth the pittance we paid, so peaceful inside and simple, quite moving to stand there in silence. I felt the spirits of the Knights in there and was moved to write in the visitor book my feelings. The structure dates back to the 12th century and is based on the octagonal church of the Holy Sepulchre in Jerusalem. The eight sided star shape of the lofty cupola is emblematic of the Knights. I picked up a leaflet of the church to take home, a pleasant respite from the weary road.

193

The fascinating history of the Knights Templar incorporates about two centuries during the Middle Ages, from the Order's founding in the early 12th century, to when it was disbanded in the early 14th century and it's a subject I'm curious to learn more about).

From Torres de Río it was a 9km slog of marching. Up and down on a gravel path, then the highway, then through farm fields. We passed almond, olive and apple trees, maybe also apricot, we were not sure as they were very small. So very hot again, took ages to find a sliver of shade were we took our boots off and had some lunch. I did not buy a sandwich for the road as I find I cannot eat a lot while hiking. Today's lunch was a peach, a kit-kat and a bottle of orange juice. We drink lots of water while walking. We saw the man with his dog again today; it is an old golden retriever. The poor thing pads along with his tongue hanging out. Skai tells me that in the garden last night the man was trying to coax the dog up some steps, in the end he had to physically lift the dogs' paws up one by one.

Our Refugio is spotlessly clean; there are four bunks in the room. Because we were early again, we snagged two bottom bunks. Later on we were joined by two elderly Chinese ladies who are carrying their gear in shopping buggies, the kind that people use here when they go grocery shopping. The Spanish lady, who showed us to our bunks, hugged us both and pushed out her face for us to kiss her on both cheeks! They are such an affable people who treat us so very well. The beds have clean white sheets so we don't need bed bug protection again. Also, despite what we were told before we left, there has been an abundance of toilet paper in clean washrooms.

After settling in and doing the laundry and shower routine, we struck out for the town. Apparently it is festival night and there was a very entertaining concert in the plaza. All the local kids were sat around on the floor, parents sat on benches at the back. There were clowns, acrobats, gymnasts, face painting and lots of music. Because of the celebration, we could not get a pilgrim meal, only tapas and wine for 1.50€. Too hungry for

tapas, we searched and found a place to get a "platter" and ordered chicken. It came with fries, peppers and some kind of croquette-either fish or cheese. Whatever it was I didn't like it so much.
Tomorrow we have decided to take a day off and will bus to Burgos.

Day 11: Burgos

Hotel Londres

Saturday, 31ˢᵗ August 2013   by bus

Disappointed or relieved? Not sure what I am feeling right now after we took the bus here. Looking at our slow progress, our physical state (at least mine) we are slow and quite obviously not going to do this whole trail in 35 days, so must pick out the sections we don't want to miss and concentrate on them. No doubt my body was ready for this break. The blister is sore, my knee is painful as are both hips and toe joints are starting to give a painful jab every once in a while. I upped the Ibuprofen to two a day now, so a rest day is in order. I felt awful guilty however sitting on the bus and seeing all the pilgrims walking. I wished I was out there with them and feel I have lost something. We found this hotel very quickly, however Skai thought the price too expensive, but I feel in no condition to wander around looking for something else. We were right next to the municipal Refugio which pilgrims on the street assured us was excellent and very clean for 5€, but 25 to a room, only stay one night and out by 8.00 a.m. is not my idea of a break and we had already agreed we would not stay at a Refugio. It cost us 27€ per night, which to my mind is not over the top and we booked for two nights despite Skai muttering she would rather have shopped around. The room is sheer luxury, twin beds with sheets again (no sleeping bag required) a private bathroom with thick thirsty towels, (no wet dry with that scant back - packing towel), so how much better can it be? Plus we are right on the Camino path, no walking around to find the trail when we set off again.
There is a marvellous cathedral and tomorrow I will walk up to see it, Brierley guide recommends it.
Since we arrived at 1.00 p.m. we had lots of time to explore the city and strolled along the many small streets adjacent to the hotel. Lunch at a nearby cafeteria for me was fried eggs and

jambon (ham) and for Skai chorizo sausage and fried eggs. At 3.00 p.m. we were ready for an ice cream before going back to the hotel for a siesta. I cannot sleep however; my hips won't let me, just too uncomfortable to lie down anymore. I watched the television instead, a cycle race, much like the Italian Giro, but I think it was the Spanish version.

It is evening now as I write and we have just come back from having tapas.

Skai seems to be faring much better than I, she seems to handle the trails well and is lively with conversation and cheerfully eager to talk with whomever we meet.

I on the other hand seem, disappointingly, to be wilting, but I am hardly surprised. Skai works energetically in her garden all summer, planting, weeding, cutting grass, gathering wild mushrooms, she walks her long driveway to her mailbox regularly, a distance there and back of some 5km. She swims in the lakes and generally is a very healthy and hardy type. This is her first backpacking adventure. Her home and garden are straight out of a magazine and her talent for all things grown; bottled or pickled is common knowledge. She is generous too and shares abundant vegetables and raspberries in season because her crops are so bountiful. As a researcher she is unsurpassed and is amazingly well read. "I should have been an actuary" she says when I ask enviously how she remembers so much detail. Reading voraciously, she retains everything, whereas I tend to be a bit of a scatter-brain.

I can't help but admire her self-discipline, she has a strict regimen and sticks to it relentlessly and I'm struck by her self-control. This is a quality I admire and seek to emulate, but never seem to be totally successful at. I can start off really well, but sooner or later, I fall off the wagon. For example:-

She will drink only red wine because she believes it is good for you

Always wear sunglasses even on a cloudy day.

Changes her focal point every twenty minutes. "When you are walking with your eyes on the ground every twenty minutes you should look up, the same applies when reading a book." Skai says and admits she always remembers to do this when reading at home. It sounds very tiresome to me and I feel I must be a hopeless cause, for I have already broken the rule. I have been looking at this journal for more than twenty minutes and I am not sure if I looked away or not.

In addition, one should drink water every 10 minutes. (I definitely don't drink enough water, they say you should drink six glasses a day, I don't)

Don't sit on the sunny side of the bus, or in the sun as sun is very unhealthy.

Always wear a sun hat.

I am the polar opposite of Skai alas and starting to feel quite slovenly in my habits. My garden is an insult to the sign at the bottom of our driveway which states I am a member of the horticultural society. I noticed a sweet pea alongside the trail today and pointed it out. It was not a sweet pea, but a perennial sweet pea; not being a gardener I thought there was only one.

I often eat the wrong foods and my love of all things chocolate is famous. I remember my ten year old grandson coming to me solemnly one day and saying very seriously as he thrust a Mars Bar into my hand "this is for all the things you do for me." I was overwhelmed; in his tender and innocent ten years, he knew already that grandma was a roll-over for chocolate. I eat too many comfort foods, like cookies, sweets and any kind of chocolate bar. Right now I'd kill for a Mars Bar, which I feel to be good for you as they contain glucose. I believe in the doctrine "A mars a day keeps the doctor away."

I think the Camino is making me face some issues that I need to attend to; such as diet, self - discipline, patience, goodwill to others and love thy neighbour stuff for I am feeling slightly unhinged.

To change the subject, I feel we need to get back on the Camino 'tout suite.'

Skai however, has decided she does not want to walk any more. This is not a total surprise; I've had this ominous feeling ever since we started. Her knee has started to hurt and she feels she should not walk on it anymore. Apparently she must bring in the winter wood at home and in fairness, this was discussed before we left Canada. We had adjusted our schedule to suit this important chore. The knee injury could be compromising her obligation. "I don't want to do permanent damage" she says. Hmmmm. I have a vision of me being left in the lurch and have very mixed feelings about that. Part of me wants to do this whole thing alone and then there is the other part that is slightly nervous about that. Am I about to be tried even further?

Day 12: Burgos

Hotel Norte y Londres

Sunday, 1st September 2013   rest day

A quiet day today, woke up at 7.30 a.m. and stayed in bed until 8.00 a.m. Not a good night's sleep again due to my right hip. Tonight I will take extra strength Tylenol instead of the Ibuprofen.

We met a German girl in the restaurant this morning who also booked a hotel stay here for a rest. I also saw the energetic young French couple from Zaraquigei and the girls leg was bandaged from thigh to ankle. Obviously they are also on a layover. Quite a few pilgrims here it seems use Burgos to recover, so suddenly I don't feel quite so bad. We are all guilty of the same mistake. We jump onto the Camino full of piss and vinegar and burn out in ten days. We all make this mistake, despite all the books warning you not to do this. Now we pay for the error of our ways. The Camino has lessons for those who listen.

Yesterday as we walked into the city centre from the bus station, a little girl, maybe three or four years old, suddenly called to her father.

"I found some" she cried.

"What did you find?" he said.

"Some pilgrims" she thrilled.

It was so cute and we all laughed, but also, made us feel like celebrities.

We both toured the cathedral, which is hugely impressive. Lots of gold on plaster figures, tapestries, oil paintings etc. But not as impressive to me as those I saw in Italy.

Tomorrow we hike 22km to Hornillos. I have arranged for our packs to be sent on ahead of us. It will also be our first day on the Meseta, let's see how we survive that.

Day 13: Hornillos

Monday; 2nd September 2013

Albergue Municipal	distance walked	Ascent 150m
32 beds	21.7km	

Today was an easy hike out of Burgos, mostly through parkland then two small villages. The Meseta is easy walking, especially without our packs. Hornillos is very small (pop 100) and the Municipal Refugio was full so we were sent down the road to an overflow building that has an additional fourteen beds. We are cramped into one tiny room, with only one toilet and the single shower is down the road at the main Refugio.

I walked partly with Mike from Dublin today and a lady from Sheffield England who returns to the Camino every year to walk for two weeks. Later on we walked with Fiona also from Dublin. There are a lot of Irish here, but the majority I would say are from Germany, with Spain running a close second. The weather was not too hot today, sunny with clear blue skies and a very gentle breeze which helped to keep us cooler.

As I sit here in the plaza I have had my shower and done my laundry, which now hangs in the garden at the back. So that at 3.45 p.m. I find myself seated on a bench on the main street of this lovely remote little hamlet sipping on a tall glass of lemonade with ice. Skai is in bed in the dorm, she is in the corner of that dark gloomy room doing a crossword puzzle. I asked her to come sit outside on a bench, but she declines on the ground it is not healthy to sit in the sun. I told her there are seats in the shade, "yes, but are they comfortable?" was the reply. I have given up, therefore I sit here with other pilgrims. I don't think she enjoyed today, her cheerful demeanor has vanished and her face is drawn and ashen. Says her knee is very bad and she does not want to do permanent damage. Wants to send the bags ahead again tomorrow, also wants to take the bus again. I, on the other hand am not ready to give up just yet. I suggested we walk only 10km to Hontanos and then review the situation. Skai agreed and I suggested she try the local masseur advertised on the information board at the refugio.

One hour later she appears from the massage parlour with weird strips of black tape over her knee and said the lady diagnosed her problem as being "in the bone" as opposed to only muscle pain. She went on to tell me that her pain tolerance is exceptionally high and that she does not take anesthesia at the dentist office. "I hate to see you" he wails "I know I hurt you." I absolutely don't know what to make of it all, pain is such a personal thing and how can one relate to another's pain? We all have differing levels of tolerance. I must be a better pilgrim and take things at face value, but I can' help feeling frustrated. She is having her pack sent on again and is considering bussing the rest of the way

I bought a microwave pasta and yogurt at the Super Mercado for dinner and ate glumly in the communal kitchen.

Pilgrim lesson today:-"Patience is a virtue which few people possess"

Day 14: Castrojerez

Albergue Casa Nostra (priv) 26 beds

Tuesday; 3rd September 2013   21.4km   ascent 250m

Skai sent her pack ahead, but I decided to carry mine and what a difference it does make. It was however another easy walking day, flat, still on the Meseta, very hot again, in fact, intensely so. After showering etc. in the Albergue, we set off to find a restaurant and even in this tiny village, at 5.00 p.m. it was still like an oven. No wonder the Spanish stay indoors and have siesta, no sign of life and all the metal blinds closed at the windows. Not a breath of wind and on the cobblestone streets, no sign of life, it was like walking through a ghost town. I sweated and puffed on the up and down streets as much as I had on the Meseta all day.

We found a lovely cottage on the main street, with a "welcome pilgrims" on the door with a complimentary dish of cookies and nuts. Inside was all tranquility; music, art on the walls, interesting books and artifacts displayed as in a small museum. There was also a lovely garden in the back, with handmade wooden crosses, lavender beds and all kinds of herbs and flowers. A bearded and very soft spoken older man, with long hair showed us some caves at the back that he was excavating. He was finding all kinds of pieces of pottery and what appeared to be a stone tunnel. He believed it to be hundreds of years old and thought it came down from an abandoned castle up on the hill behind the village. He had found lots of gypsum and gave us both some.

Met Robin and Bill from California, who had hooked up with Nellie from Denmark, all three were hiking together. They are extremely fit, Robin is celebrating his 75th birthday next year and this is his gift to self. They walk fast and will for sure complete this trail in 35 days. The rest of the women (four French women) were also hiking together and they had huge suitcases with them which were being transported by van every day. They carried only small day packs each day. Not sure how far they were going, they kept mostly to themselves. Robin expressed disdain at the French ladies. There are some "pilgrims" on the road who are walking with support vehicles and not carrying packs. The vans meet them at specific points with packed lunches, bottled water and a chance to ride in the van if you choose. These luxuries are viewed with scorn by the purist pilgrims who walk and suffer the whole way with no support at all, which is after all, what a pilgrimage is.

Day 15: Leon

Hostal Albany

Wednesday 4th September, 2013   bus

At Castrojerez, it was back to the bus again. The next day's section started with another big climb, so we decided to avoid it by taking the bus to Leon. I am not exactly stellar, disappointed with my performance and not happy about the number of times we are taking the bus and sitting in hotels.

We left the Albergue at 7.15 a.m. and headed for the local bus stop. It was a cool morning and we had a 45minute wait at the stop, which is merely a crude shelter on the street. A huge German Shepard dog is thankfully behind a wrought iron fence; otherwise I am sure he would have had us for breakfast. We had to go back to Burgos in order to make the connection to Leon. After buying our tickets to Leon we went into the station for breakfast. I laid the ticket on the table and Skai agreed to wait there while I went to the counter. Since we had an hour to wait, I ordered my usual café con leche and an almond croissant and went back to Skai at the table and then we instantly decided to move to a window table. Skai went and got her breakfast and then we sat and relaxed a good twenty minutes. Because Skai wanted a bank machine and does not want to walk on her knee too much, I went out into the street to locate one; I also found a candy store where I bought chocolate bars for the bus. As Skai went to the bank machine I sat talking to two ladies from Germany. Meanwhile, the café was bustling with business and the two girls at the counter were overwhelmed, making espressos, serving sandwiches etc. Finally our bus came in and we went to the platform to board. That's when I remembered my ticket. I couldn't remember where I had put it; I searched pockets, day pack, everywhere to no avail. In desperation, I ran to an information office and told him "billet perdido" which according to my phrase book means 'ticket lost'. He just shrugged his shoulders and waved me away, pointing to the cashier. I was mortified, he couldn't care less. I then ran to the cashier, which now had a long line-up of passengers buying tickets. At 10.27 a.m. I finally got to the counter and offered 50€ to purchase another ticket to Leon. But all he would say is "completo" which meant the bus was full and no more tickets were available. I tried desperately to tell him I had a ticket but it was "perdido" and even gave him my seat number. But he kept waving me away and the Spanish man behind me said "he wants you to go and sit down!" I have never been so stressed and then it dawned on me, I had put my ticket on that first table. I ran back into the café, to the table where we had first sat and was now covered in dirty plates, cups and saucers. I moved them all away and there was my ticket. Hallelujah, a miracle! How is it possible that no one took that ticket? It didn't have my name on it, there are many people just loitering around the station. Anyone wanting to go to Leon had a free ticket and the bus was full, so obviously lots of people go there. I was still feeling unhinged when we boarded the bus and I swore to be more careful next time. We met Maria, from Galway, Ireland, on the bus and when I told her what had happened she said "that's how the Camino works." An Angel on my shoulder again. Maria also is bussing today. But she will do better than us on the Camino, she says she is very fit and walks 30km every day. She also plans to walk to Finisterre. We had a lovely conversation, especially about Nora O'Faolain and her book "Are you Somebody?" Maria had also listened to that famous last interview with O'Faolain and said it was riveting. I have to try and find that. Think I have the transcript in my eBook. We bid fond farewell to Maria in Leon then hiked through town to this lovely hostel directly across from the Cathedral. The weather is 29°, clear blue skies with lots of sunshine.

After taking the bus Skai seems much better and back to her bubbly self. We have found an elegant restaurant for dinner and sit back to enjoy a pleasant meal. Skai orders her red wine and I try a Spanish beer.

Day 16: Villandangos del Paramo

Albergue Municipal 72 beds

| Thursday, September 5th, 2013 | distance walked 23.4km | Ascent.nil |

We left Leon at 8.45 a.m. which is far too late. As pilgrims we suck! The plan was to hike to Virgen del Camino (8km) stay overnight, then hike to Mazarife tomorrow thus enabling Skai to have more opportunity to rest her knee again. But my suspicions came true when Skai insisted her knee was worse, declined to take one of my extra strength Tylenol, or knee ointment and at Virgen del Camino insisted we stop and she see a doctor. We were directed to a clinic in a side street and sat in the waiting room which already had a small line-up. After an hour, she finally saw a doctor then emerged joyful that he had given her a hip injection and told her to rest for two days. My heart sank, we have spent three of the last five days lounging around and now we have to sit for another two. She has indicated again she would like to bus the rest of the way, but there is no way I am going to commit to that. I felt completely frustrated, it was 11.30 a.m. and I can't stand another day in a hotel with the television, so I decided to carry on and set off angrily to walk the next 15.4km alone. Just five minutes later and on the edge of town, the sky turned ink black, there was thunder and in the distance lightning (was I being punished for my lack of patience?) Almost immediately the heavens opened. I ran for cover to the side of a factory building to put on my rain gear and cover my pack, then in a torrential monsoon, marched along the highway down to a grass track. The trail instantly turned to that thick muddy clay that Brierley talks about, red thick clay that sticks to your boots. I was instantly five inches taller. Filled with utter foreboding, I felt very unsure if I was right to continue on, or perhaps should turn back. There was not a soul to be seen either in front or behind me and in minutes I was thoroughly drenched, pants soaked and sticking to my legs. Next a flash of lightning and the loudest clap of thunder right over my head threatened to heap untold vengeance on me. The storm was moving quickly and was soon over my head, then in one long booming clap rolled right on by. The rain continued however and quite suddenly I found myself at the tunnel that goes under the A61. Huddled together inside were four pilgrims, rain had made a small river in the tunnel so I could get the clay off my boots. It was a relief to find some real live people. I dragged out my Brierley to check where I was, as I needed to take a turn soon to go to Mazarife. One of the pilgrims, a young man from Texas came over to look at the guide also, he pointed to Valandangos del Paramo where they were all going and I pointed to Mazarife where I was going. But looking at the guide, I saw that I had missed my turn-off and was also going towards Valandangos. This turned out to be a happy mistake, as the route was a single track running alongside the highway, flat as a pancake all the way. The rain never stopped and I promised myself a hotel with a bath and laundry facilities when I got there. But this was not to be, the only accommodation was the municipal Albergue for 5€ per night and for another 5€ there was a washing machine available.

By 3.30 p.m. I am showered, changed, my laundry (everything) is in the washing machine and I comfortably ensconced in my lower bunk. I feel smug with myself that I had done so well, all things considered and decided I was very happy to be travelling alone. The two female staff here are extremely helpful and friendly, the dorm is very spacious with eighteen bunk beds. It is very quiet as I lie here writing. Only nine bunks are occupied at the moment, most people are sleeping, one is reading and this one is writing. The sun has come out and one of the ladies has brought me my washing, she leads me out to the garden at the back where everything is hung in brilliant sunshine on an empty clothesline. I'm crossing my fingers everything dries. I have looked at my Brierley guide for tomorrow and there is no option but to continue along the N120 to Hospital de Orbigo and that is only 11km, so let's see how I cope with that. My left knee is still extremely sore, right toe joint is paining me and will tell you about the hips as soon as I try to sleep tonight.

Pilgrim meal is squash soup, a leg of chicken and a bottle of water. None of it good, all frozen and micro-waved (except the water of course.) I couldn't eat very much; the chicken too greasy, so in future I will buy my own food. There is usually a kitchen available and I can then eat at the time I want instead of having to wait until seven or eight at night.

I sat with three girls at dinner; Melinda from Calgary, Anda from Germany and Sarah from Sydney. It was a casual evening with much friendly chatter comparing our experiences so far on the trail.

Day 17: Hospital de Orbigo

Albergue San Miguel 40 Beds

Friday; 6ᵗʰ September 2013   11.5km.   Ascent nil

I left this morning at 7.20a.m after fishing around in the dark trying to pack my stuff and not finding the bag for the bed bug sheet. I finally pushed everything in my pack and checked several times with my head-lamp that I had not left anything behind. It must be in the pack somewhere.

Although I hate to admit it, even to myself, my left knee and right hip are both extremely sore today. I don't want, in the worst, way to quit.

I walked alone along a small gravel path beside the N120. Sometimes going into the trees; other times just an open path. At 8.20a.m. I walked into San Martin del Camino-that's one hour for 4.7km! Despite a gammy knee, I did one of my personal fastest times, but I have consistently worn the knee brace which is my saviour. I stopped into Albergue Veira for a coffee and a cookie and to use their washroom. Again, a sincere welcome to a complete stranger and the cost, just 1€. This was my first meal as I didn't want to have anything at the hostel. I like the routine of walking for an hour, then stopping. There is almost always some lovely little roadside bar or café that has café con leche and fresh pastries. I was hoping to find such a place this morning, but it is pretty meagre along this highway, I was dying for an almond croissant. But is was not to be today, so I pressed on to Hospital de Orbigo, stopping just twice; once to take off the long sleeve T-shirt, as the sun was up and I was hot, then briefly behind a cow shed for a pit stop. Cyclists going by always ring their bells and scare the living daylights out of you, they approach so fast out of nowhere and they zoom past on the narrow path. As I sat on the grass, having stuffed my T-shirt into my pack, motorists beeped and cyclists yelled "Buen Camino" and I allowed myself to sit there and wallow in a stolen moment of self-conceit.

At 11.00 a.m. I walked into Hospital de Orbigo, absolutely flabbergasted. I didn't expect to get here this early in the day. I averaged 3.3km per hour, probably better if you take out the stops and breakfast at the Albergue. Mind you it was flat all the way, but my pack was a bit heavier because I put all the contents of my day pack in it also instead of carrying it separately at the front. At the entrance to the village I crossed the hugely long Puente de Orbigo, which dates back to the 13th century and is one of the longest and best preserved medieval bridges in Spain. Jousting tournaments took place here in 1434. A noble knight from Leon issued the challenge to every knight who tried to cross the bridge. He successfully defended the bridge and broke 300 lances in the course of the requisite one month. Apparently that was the required thing do if he was to regain his honour after being scorned by a certain beautiful lady.

I sat for a while to contemplate my next move. I feel like staying in a private Albergue and decided to look for the Verde Privee; I walked past a hotel; a hostel then the parish hostel but no sign of the Verde. It was exactly 10.55a.m. when I saw two pilgrims waiting outside the San Miguel Albergue on the main street and decided not to go further. Since I am feeling tired and worn I have been weighing my options from this point on. After much thought and soul searching have decided to take a bus tomorrow to Astorga, then maybe bus again to Sarria. This decision is painful, I had such dreams of walking every inch, I really thought I could, but now I must accept that I will not. My knee has become much more painful even when I stop walking and my hips are stinging with every step. Perhaps if I sent the pack ahead it might help, but the truth is, right now I am simply tired. The two pilgrims are elderly folks like me from Germany and they say the Albergue will open in five minutes. At exactly 11.00a.m. we were welcomed in and signed up, then shown to the dorm. The Albergue is very serene and spacious with a large kitchen and lovely garden that has lots of tables and chairs. Up one flight (why are they always up a flight of stairs?) is the dorm with wooden bunks, all neatly made up in orange and yellow plaid coverlets. I picked a bed tucked into a corner and close to the washrooms. As I was arranging my pack and sleeping bag, I overheard the two Germans talking to someone who said she was from Canada, so I went to introduce myself to, you guessed it, yes, Skai! I was dumb founded and asked her how come she was here. She said she had emailed me to say I should meet her here. But of course, I had not been anywhere near a computer since I left her in Virgen del Camino. My heart fell to my boots, talk about fate. Seems she had jumped straight on a bus when I left her and came here, telling the hosts she had doctor's orders to rest. Normally, one cannot stay more than one night without a Doctor's Note. She has been in bed for two days, says her knee is still too painful to walk and the injection he gave her was no help. Maria from Ireland was here last night who cooked supper for her as she only gets out of bed now to go to the washroom. She asked me to hang out her laundry for her and get her something to eat for lunch. For some reason a vague feeling of doom just swept over me.

I showered and then walked out to find the bus station to check on the schedule for tomorrow. There are several busses to Astorga tomorrow. I am hoping to catch a bus at 10.00a.m. I have already made up my mind to bus to Sarria. My knee needs to rest a bit and I think I can do the last 100km very slowly, with rest days where possible. Next I went to the tiny Super Mercado to get lunch for us both and happened upon the deli counter. I asked the Spanish lady if I could get a Boccadillo. At this she produced a huge fresh baguette and nodded. I replied "Si." She cut it in half and slicing it asked me to pick out what I wanted in it. I pointed to the ham and she just loaded each half. The forty something blue-eyed, blond and athletic German man, who just an hour ago was prancing around his bunk next to me in his very brief underwear, came up and said "Did you just ask for that ya?"

"Si" I grinned back.

"You are very smart, I want one also"
And as the lady was piling ham on to the second half, he
whispered to me, "Now if we could have Tomato with that"
I replied I didn't know the Spanish for Tomato, at which the
Senora said, "I know what you say" and she walked over and
picked out the biggest juiciest looking tomato. "Fresh, local"
she beamed.
So there I had this enormous sandwich and my German buddy
was positively beguiled. As I was handed two big foil wrapped
packages, my buddy looked at me and smiled "Big sandwich
for a little lady."
Who would have known that a trip to the Super Mercado could
be so much fun? I took Skai her sandwich, banana and yogurt
to eat in bed and then went down to the garden, along with my
new German friend and his buddy. As they each opened foil
parcels my friend called over to me "I wish you a good lunch."
For some reason, a stocky and elderly Spanish lady who
apparently works here, seemed equally impressed with the
sandwich, for as she passed by my table she let out a string of
Spanish and gave me a big thumbs up, only to repeat it all again
as she went by a second time, only this time I got two thumbs
up and more Spanish. She came back a third time, grabbed my
hand and gave it a vigorous shake, laughing and babbling in
Spanish: to this day I have no idea what she said. I do wish I
knew, in fact she has just gone by again and given me the biggest
smile and another thumbs up. I am sitting with Connie from
Denmark. "Do you know what she's talking about?" I asked.
Connie has no idea either. I get someone to take a picture of me
with this famous sandwich.
I sat and talked with Connie for over an hour, although from
Denmark, she has flawless English. Then pleasantly stuffed,
returned to the dorm and fell asleep in my bunk. My new friend
from Germany took a Siesta too and his feet meet up with my
face exactly. We both awoke at the same time and he sent me a
little wave.

It is now 5.40 p.m. and I have decided not to eat a big meal tonight. I have an orange and an apple; I have potato chips and Pepsi. I find I cannot eat large meals and that sandwich was very filling.

Now a note to self; when reading this at home, remember, everything sounds rather idyllic, BUT, my knee is intensely sore, my hips also, I am quite tired and I still have 120km of strenuous walking ahead of me plus some serious climbs again. This trip cannot be planned as a whole. One can only do one day at a time. It's impossible to predict how you will feel at any given time, what the weather will be like, or which body parts will fail. Many pilgrims have knee and hip problems, I've seen legs bandaged thigh to ankle, scabbed knees and faces, black eyes (falling on cobble stone streets). People with blisters laid up for days. Torn tendons, lots of people fail the Camino; some have even died, as evidenced by the several grave markers on the trail. At this point, Skai is an unknown quantity, I suspect she will not finish.

Two new pilgrims came in and sat at the next table, Ann and Mike are from Manchester. They are on a two week cycle holiday. Despite my earlier promise to myself, I went for supper with them, as Mike said they found a place round the corner that serves Egg and Chips. We laughed so much; it was down a side street, at a really cosy bar with a restaurant in the back. Sure enough, menu pictures over the bar showed menu item "#3", a picture of a plate of egg and chips. "We don't even have to speak Spanish" said Mike, just point to the picture. Mike and Ann asked if they could buy me a drink and we all had beer. Just as we sat in the restaurant, we noticed Connie and Angela (she is from Colorado) so we ended up joining them. What a super time we had, Mike has that great British dry humour which I have missed for so long, we had a long night eating and discussing such a wide range of subjects. For some unknown reason I spoke of that nightmare of a trip with BJ in Algonquin and Angela had some really insightful observations on the many avenues of human psychology. She works in Mental Health and has worked with many addictive problems. For such a young girl, I had found her deeply compassionate and knowledgeable. Not that the talk was all heavy, quite the opposite, with Mike and Anne bringing the British slant of humour to everything, it was the best night I have had since starting the Camino nearly three weeks ago.

We sauntered back through the cobblestone streets at 8.45 p.m. which is late for us, most pilgrims are in bed and asleep by 9.00 p.m. and everything is quiet.

Diane Campbell Thompson

Day 18: Ponferrada

Hotel Madrid

Saturday, 7th September 2013.   Bus

After reading the Brierley guide, I decided I must see the Knight Templar Castle at Ponferada and at the last minute did a quick change to go there instead of Sarria, so this is where I am now! Skai was up ahead of me this morning and enjoying a convivial breakfast with Mike and Ann before we set off for the bus station. They were all in deep discussion on the price of petrol in England. Skai had enquired the price and was busy computing pounds into Canadian dollars which she says was $1.37 according to the previous day papers, but probably closer to $1.41 if you were actually buying pounds and not selling them, at which Mike said it was far too complicated a subject for breakfast and we all with furrowed brows breathed a sigh of relief and fell back into our coffee.

As we left the bus station, I stopped a Peregrina and asked her if she knew of an Albergue nearby. She was German and immediately said "Don't stay in any Albergue." She was covered in bed bug bites and said today they were much better; yesterday they were all over her body and face. She said she was on her way home, visibly upset, saying they were probably in her pack too. I felt so sorry for her, another pilgrim that has their hopes dashed. I've seen it all just about, bandages, black eyes, bruises, scrapes and just about everyone has a knee brace, sometimes two. Many Germans are wearing now a new knee band, which is just a tight black band that goes either just above the knee or below it. If I can find one I intend to try it, they say it works better than the regular knee brace. As I came out of the bus station, something snapped in the side of my right knee, felt like a sharp knife stab and gets me with every step. I needed that knee; it was the only good one I had left!

Here at the Hotel Madrid I am feeling guilty in sheer luxury once again, with soap, shampoo, towels, a bidet, a lovely deep bath tub and a television we do not understand.

Once again I go exploring the city and find the Knights Templar Castle. So worth the walk, I was able to get inside and it is huge, with tiny slits to shoot arrows out of, lots of great round parapets. It's amazing to survey the huge structure of pile upon pile of stones and try to imagine the work involved to build such magnificence. Out alongside the castle, there's a busy street market lined with outdoor cafes; stalls of artisan crafts, pottery, leather, beautiful Spanish dresses, piles of fresh baked cobs of bread, barrels of olives. It was a great atmosphere; I strolled along eating a mango ice cream and generally spending a pleasant three hours there. I hated to go back to the room, but my knee dictated an end to strolling.

It's Festival weekend! Fireworks all night long! Dancing in the street, loud music! The Spaniards are nocturnal and in a party mood; they sleep all day and come alive at night. I would love to have joined in, but my knee is hurting and I don't really feel like partying alone, although I doubt I would be alone too long, the streets are full of crowds.

Day 19: Sarria

Gas station motel on the edge of town

Sunday, 8th September 2013   by bus

We left the hotel at 11.00 a.m. and ten minutes later found us at the bus station again. As I walked into the bus station I got a sudden sharp pain that cut clean across my left knee, now I can barely put weight on it. Just what I need, it's such a drag and I need my legs right now.

Anyway, boarding the bus to Lugo was smooth and efficient and the connection to Sarria was right there on the same platform and it turned out to be a very short ride. Apparently there is festival here also, so all accommodation is full. A very young receptionist offered to call to a pension in the country. It is 4km out of town, there is a free pickup and return and the cost per night is 35€. Well, there really isn't any other choice and it seems a fair deal, but the "pension in the country" turned out to be a gas station and truck stop. The room however was just fine and again a private bathroom. The receptionist also sold me some cooling knee cream. I would kill for an ice pack but that seems to be right out of the question and the cooling cream feels good on my knee which is burning hot. Tomorrow there will be a room available at the hotel so we are booked there. The young girl on the reception desk was extremely helpful and suggested I send my pack on from here to Santiago. Looks like I must do this as my knee is about done for now, acutely painful now, with a sharp stabbing pain with every step.

Went back to the room to write some postcards, write my journal, eat a mars bar and have a nap while Skai watched a Spanish soap opera on the television.

Day 20: Sarria

Hotel Villa de Sarria

Monday, 9th September 2013   no walking

*"I'm not enjoying this" Skai says suddenly after our transfer
back to the hotel in Sarria. "I'm going home" she says.*
*This does not come as a complete surprise; she came along on
the bus but has refused to walk for the last five days.*
*Everything happens quickly now, Skai booked a train ticket to
Madrid and was gone within the hour. I have decided I am going
to try and get to Santiago come hell or high water.*
*I have just given the receptionist my list for the baggage transfer
and have spread a seven day hike into 14! My knee is in such bad
shape I dare not try long distances; I have broken the route into
small manageable hikes. The worse thing that can happen is I
will have to take a bus, but I am clinging to the hope I can walk
all the way. I have rested my knee all day today, took an Arthotec
that Dr. Gauthier gave me for pain, this was my pain killer of
last resort and I will take another at bedtime tonight. Am still
experimenting with a cocktail of pain killers and Ibuprofen to
find out what works best.*
*The cost to send my pack to the end is 42€, which is very
reasonable I think. I see some people take colossal pieces of
luggage, I mean suitcases. Pilgrims with packs look at these
people with a certain amount of disdain. I feel guilty for not
carrying my pack all the way.*
*I will admit to being nervous at setting off alone, hoping not to
get lost is my first concern, my knee is the second. But I must
at least give it a try. So God willin' and the creek don't rise, I
will get to Santiago, the outcome rests with fate. I always really
wanted to do this alone, time to put my money where my mouth
is and also to exercise a little faith in the future.*

Day 21: Barbedelo

Casa Barbedelo. Priv. 23 beds

Tuesday, 10th September, 2013   5.2km

A bright and sunny day and I followed a beautiful rural footpath through ancient woodlands of oak and chestnut, over old stone bridges, along quiet country roads dotted with a few serious uphill climbs. There are several huffing and puffing pilgrims on the road too. I arrived here just after noon as I deliberately walked slowly and truly enjoyed the scenery. I ordered a café con leche (pekenya i.e.small) as soon as I got here, then paid for my room which is 45€. It's a bit steep, but I'll not complain, I have a large room and bathroom all to myself and I consider it my reward for bravery today as I was quite nervous when I set out.

However, I am now sitting on a chaise lounge and have been chatting with a lady from South Africa. This is like a motel unit and the view from this chair is magnificent, distant green hills dotted with small hamlets. I feel quite at peace after a very leisurely and happy walk today. I need to find an ATM in a hurry tomorrow, as I paid cash for this room and cash for my bags, so I am down to 170€. I expect somewhere in the next two days I shall find one. At the moment as I sit here, I am very happy to have decided to go on.

Met up with Maria again from Ireland, we sat and chatted for a long while, she is going to a pilgrim mass with three others tonight and invited me to go along, they are all going out for dinner afterwards. I declined because; a) the mass is down the road another km and not sure I should push my knee and b) that means they will be eating about 9.00 p.m. which is too late for me.

Instead I opted to go to the restaurant for a ham and cheese sandwich and also bought fruit for tomorrow. I joined three others, Michelle from New Zealand, Marize (who is 88) and

her son Bruce, from California. They all started in Sarria as I did and Bruce is going extra slow to accommodate his mom. We had a lot of fun at the table, talking about music and movies and Michelle has a hilarious sense of humour.
Went back to my room at 7.30 p.m. as I feel my knee starting up again, but I have not taken any meds today.

Day 22: Morgade

Casa Morgade, Priv 6 beds

Wednesday, 11th September 2013   7.8km

Had a relaxed start at ten to eight with just one coffee and banana before I left. Again, another beautiful walk, peaceful and pastoral, some ups and down, chestnut groves and small hamlets that melt seamlessly into each other. Sensory perception seems more alive with the smells of fresh cow dung and hay, the sounds chickens crowing, cows mooing and the clip clop of horses being lead to new pastures. Sights, sounds and smells that hitherto seem to have been lost or forgotten. Two pilgrims just ahead of me fed a couple of the horses with apples that had fallen from a nearby tree. The horses loved them and crunched loudly and hungrily. Plodding just one step in front of the other, I amble along, soaking everything in. Even so, I arrived at the Albergue in three hours. I really could have gone on to Portomarin had I known how easy this would be. Still, I prefer to linger here in rural Spain, than spend extra days in Santiago. A big party of Irish here today, Casa Morgade is a busy rest stop, like Union Station at times. My pack arrived one and half hours after me and happily I see it is tagged all the way to Santiago. My room is private again, but as with last night, they seem to think I ordered a double room. I think the hotel assumed Skai would be with me when they made the reservations. Today the cost was 28€ so I shall run out of cash if this keeps up. I could use a better day pack, I was not prepared for one and this one is really just a fold out shopping bag with shoulder straps. I am going to have to make do with it.

Two groups on horseback went by today and I took several pictures. The lense on my camera keeps sticking and sometimes will not open. I kept poking it and finally it opened, but I hope I don't have a camera problem; I want to take pictures in Santiago.

The weather has been perfect, clear blue skies and a slight breeze that keeps you just the right temperature.

I'm finding I like being alone, sometimes a group will catch up with me, all babbling so loud and trying to talk over each other. They are mostly younger pilgrims and many are Spanish. I find they talk very loud. I let them pass by and once again I am in silence with only the sounds of nature to listen to. I sometimes wonder, what does one find to talk about so incessantly?

It is only 1.30p.m. I have all afternoon to lounge. I am hoping the weather holds out and I can continue this leisurely pace. As I sit here in the courtyard, a herd of cows has just gone by, all complaining loudly about something. Two ladies from Quebec joined me, they are also moving at a snail's pace as one has diabetes.

Diane Campbell Thompson

Day 23: Portomarin

Albergue O'Mirador, Priv 22beds.

Thursday, 12th September 2013   11.9 km

Left in a cool mist at 8.00a.m.with yet another gorgeous walk through many small hamlets again, arriving at the Meccadoire at 10.30 and the steep steps up to Portomarin at 11.30a.m. Found an ATM on the main street to get another 200€, so I hope this sees me to the end.
Tomorrows hike is about the same distance as today but I shall not stay at an Albergue and have booked a pension. This place is very good, the dorms small and neat. My roommates are Mary from Cornwall, Phil from Germany, an Alec Guinness look alike from Australia and a young couple who are in bed together behind a towel they have draped over the edge. Alec is not impressed with them. By 12.30p.m. I was showered and laundered so headed off to check out the town. Beautiful clean place, the main street is lined with shops, lot of souvenir shops and outdoor cafes. After an afternoon siesta, I went out to the patio and ordered pork chops, with French fries and a fried egg, with a bottle of Fanta to drink. It was delicious and the first time in a while I have felt like eating a big meal. In the evening, we four went down to the bar for a drink and sat talking for hours. We have no idea what the young couple are up to.

Day 24: Hospital

Pension El Labrador

13th September 2013   11.4 km

It was a little tiring today as we are climbing all the time, steeply at first, then subtly ever since. But still there are the same lovely vista and country paths, but not so many hamlets. As I left Portomarin, we are like a great army, troops of pilgrims all marching in the same direction. Eventually we all spread out and at the back, me and my shadow in serene solitude. Lots of bird song; strong country aromas, some quite rancid actually and a dog barking somewhere in the distance.

I stopped in Gonzar for toast and coffee and met Phil and Mary. Then back on the trail to amble along again, drinking in the scenery and atmosphere of rural Spain. I feel my true Camino started only four days ago when I started out alone, it's so liberating to be free and independent and at peace. I walk in delightful spiritual aura.

It is 3.00 p.m. I have sat on this sunny terrace since arriving, leaving only briefly to take my pack to my room, which is lovely. A single bed, fresh white towels and private bathroom and expansive shower and bathtub down the hall.

The view from this terrace again looks across the landscape to green hills and valleys.

Today in the forest I passed a pilgrim sleeping on a bench, looks like she/he had been there all night. I wanted to take a picture but thought better of it. I met with the two ladies from Quebec on the path again.

Day 25: Portos

Albergue Casa A Calzada, 10 beds

Saturday, 14th September 2013   7.9km   Ascent 450m.

It is 1.20 p.m. and I am sitting in this absolutely peaceful garden. My pack arrived about one hour ago, much to my great relief. There are only two of us staying in this little corner of heaven. My fellow pilgrim is a tall older man who has indicated he does not speak. We have an unspoken bond and exchange quiet nods and smiles as we pass each other. Only song birds and the occasional rooster break the silence. The weather is warm; the sun is shining, in fact a perfect summer day. The Albergue is built of ancient stones and sits back from the road to the side of this expansive garden retreat. We are right on the main rural road and I see many pilgrims passing by. Too bad many press on to larger centres, although I am rather glad they do, I like our solitude. The dorm itself has ten beds, spacious, clean and extremely friendly. There is a small bar and café at the main bungalow, which sits close to the road, I intend to go later for supper. My laundry has been done and is hanging on the line; I had a refreshing shower, so once again I am renewed.

I left this morning in a heavy mist, but it was not really cold. I stopped for breakfast in Palais de Rei and had a very nice break with two Australian ladies. I sauntered through several small hamlets and met Mildred again from Calgary and Sarah from Australia. Later, while sitting on the patio, Anda from Germany went plodding by, still with her large wooden staff stabbing the ground determinedly with every step. She waved and grinned as on her way to Santiago she went. I also had a lovely stop in Ligonde where I got an extra stamp for my passport and was offered donativo refreshments. The Spanish are so very helpful and encouraging.

Marci writes that I should sketch for her, which is such a great idea and today I will start. I can't get over this lovely oasis and am so pleased I have decided to do short hikes and stay in rural hamlets as opposed to large centres.

I also walked part of the way with a man from Stockton-on Tees, whose son plays football for North Ferriby. We had a good laugh about Grimsby Town Football Club who apparently is worse than ever. He said it is the only Football club that never plays on home ground, but they used to I'm sure, because they (the Grimsby fans) used to chase Doncaster fans all the way back to the train station, (at least that is what someone once told me)!

I sit at this rough-hewn wooden picnic table and my book is sticking to the sap and the ever present Spanish flies are all fighting for a landing spot on my body.

A Korean man (Park is his name) has joined our little party, we are now a trio. I had supper with Park and the quiet man, who I believe to be French. The Frenchman smiled and nodded as Park and I had a long lovely talk about the Camino. Park is very religious and he has written a Korean prayer in my journal. It looks like Chinese writing, more calligraphy than writing as we know it.

It has taken me all day to figure out our silent friend is under an oath of silence. He indicates to our host to take our pictures together and we three sit smiling broadly as we huddle on the bench together at the dinner table. How blessed am I to be here and mindful that I seek and find an altered state of mind.

I have made a sketch of our dorm, which I am pleased with. At night, we three retire to our cots, by nine o'clock we are snuggled in sleeping bags, all is quiet and dark and it has been such a pleasant day again. Both men leave early in the morning.

Diane Campbell Thompson

Day 26: San Xulian

O Abrigadoiro Priv. 18 beds

Sunday, 15th September 2013 9km ascent mostly flat
some slight gains

*Today I crossed several shallow river valleys before disappearing
into the woods again to arrive at this quiet village. Again, the
only sounds are the clucking of hens, five actually, who are
walking down the centre of this village lane. The Refugio is
again, right on the path and is a small low building built entirely
of stone, with walls that measure a full 12 inches thick. It is
spotlessly clean and the hospitaleras are warm and welcoming.
It is not yet noon and I have done the usual laundry, the washing
line is out on the road, one off those small frame jobs people
have on their balconies at home. I showered and changed, made
up my bunk and am now sitting at a table to the side of the road
with my journal. My view is of stone cottages, black tile roofs,
a wooden granary and a stone cross which occupies the centre
of the very small square. My bag has just miraculously arrived
and I say it is a miracle, because no one was around when I left
this morning, so I just left it on the patio of the Refugio.
The café here has just opened; they have switched the radio on
to BBC world service with Spanish translation. We have lovely
classical music wafting towards us and I later learn that the
owners' daughter is an opera singer, who has been known to
be aired on this program.
This being Sunday, nothing is open, all seems empty and quiet.
As I walked out of Palais de Rei, an old man beckoned me into
a church to stamp my passport. It was a scene inside of instant
reverence and peace, some very soft music was playing and as
I walked towards the alter I suddenly found myself dissolving
instantly into tears. It seemed to be such a wonderful place of
sanctuary that the emotion took me completely by surprise. For
suddenly all that had happened since I had left Canada came*

228

flooding over me and I became instantly overwhelmed by it all.
I sat in reflection on how hard I had found the first week, the
pain and the sheer exhaustion, then the frustration with Skai, the
doubt about finishing alone and now being in such a peaceful
place. I finally got up to leave, with tears streaming down my
face, to the puzzlement of the kindly old man who had invited me
in. The Camino is such a deeply personal journey and to me very
much a spiritual one. I consider this experience to be a great
privilege and the difficulty will be in trying to keep this frame
of mind when I return back home and to the life I had before.

Starting out alone from Sarria, walking through hamlets,
country lanes, shaded woodland paths and sleeping in simple
rural Refugio's has been one of the wisest things I have done in
my life so far. My knee is quite sore today so I must try and rest
a bit more if possible. Tomorrows hike will be about the same
distance as today as I head to the town of Melide.

Two young Spanish girls were sitting by the path today; one
had a very bad ankle sprain. I gave her some cool-gel and a
single dose package for later. She was very grateful and said
the cooling effect was helpful, but my Spanish is poor, no better
than the first day I arrived in this country and I could offer not
a single word of comfort.

There is another group of Irish here tonight; they are a happy
bunch, laughing and joking and the life of the party. As I sat on
the patio with my journal, one of the men (Terry) came out of
the bar with two glasses of white wine, plonked one in front of
me and sat beside me. He was quickly joined with his partner in
crime, Mick. They are from Belfast; the conversation went all
over the place. Mick talked at length about the "troubles" and
I learnt a lot from him, it was a good education, information
and opinions that I was not previously aware of. Some of the
other Irish party joined us and they argued, but not angrily, so
I heard both sides of the problem very clearly. Mick and Terry
are both middle aged and married; Mick is doing the Camino
for a second time. Of course they are funny, aren't all Irish jolly?
Their waggish easy laugh, so genial and spontaneous would

229

cause even ice to melt. They asked why I was alone and I related all that had happened. "You mean you've been dumped?" Mick shouted. Then quickly gave my camera to a German man sitting nearby, "Here, take our picture" he said. Then both men snuggled up putting their arms around me. "Send this to your friend" he said, "Tell her we all slept together last night." Many others of his compatriots joined us for an afternoon of wine, song and outrageous glee. The crowd was extremely funny and I sat with them all afternoon, as we put the world to rights then back again.

Day 27: Melide

Pension Continente

Monday, September 16th, 2013   11.5km   Ascent 115m

I did a very foolish thing this morning and left far too early in the dark. There were three very rude and loud pilgrims in the adjoining bunks to me who made a hell of a racket at six o'clock. Heavy whispering, lots of zippers being pulled this way and that, climbing up and down bunk ladders and the clumsy Neanderthal who slept above me swinging first on the bunk then off again, like a blundering ape. All I could do was lie there and stare at the ceiling; finally they left, going down the cobblestone road, poles clicking and chattering gaily for all to hear. It felt like an eternity just lying there in the dark, so finally I got up and headed out at what I thought was 8.30 a.m. Not so babe; it was only 7.30 a.m. so back into the room I trundled when suddenly I heard a very noisy bunch of Spanish students coming along. They all had flashlights or head lamps, so I thought, yep, this is easy, I will just tag along with them. They were yakking away so loud over each other, no one noticed me at the back of the crowd. Well to think I could keep up with such a young energetic crowd was tantamount to thinking I could climb Everest in running shoes. Within minutes, I was left in their dust and blind as a bat in the pitch black. I tried tapping the ground to get a feel of where the path was, I knew we were in a thick forest, but the ground was very uneven, large boulders, smooth, but crooked as a dog's hind leg. It is the miracle of the day that I did not fall and break my neck. To say I was deeply regretting that decision would be a gross understatement, it was nerve wracking for more than an hour. And to think, only yesterday I resolved to be more mindful since I was told someone on the trail was robbed at gun point and I here next morning deep in the forest, pitch black, groping along, totally disoriented. Never will I set out in the dark again, I've never been so thankful to see the sun come up. In lieu of the afore mentioned robbery, I had hidden money in my boots and credit cards in my first aid kit and decided I was not going to part with them willingly. Tomorrow however, I will wait until it's light outside.

Apart from that piece of excitement, today was extremely boring and arduous, I did not enjoy this walk, mostly along a gravel road that seemed to go on forever and mostly uphill all the way. No pretty scenery as yesterday and only one small hamlet just outside of Melide.

My room is lovely, but this pension is way off the main drag and the area a bit dodgy. My bag was late arriving, well after 1.00 p.m. and I began to fret but shouldn't have, for the system is very well organized. I spent most of the afternoon in bed resting my leg. My knee was not so bad today, but now I've stopped it's throbbing like heck and is very hot to touch. The ArthoTec I took last night seemed to work and I only took one (since yesterday) and the maximum dose is two.

As soon as I had showered, I went down to the restaurant to eat, it was 4.00 p.m. CLOSED! Of course it's closed, silly me, one can never get food until 8.00 p.m. I don't know how the Spaniards manage to wait so long, I am starving already. I walked to the town centre, the restaurants are open but not cooking just yet. I checked out one place and ordered a coke and sat to survey the system, to see if anyone was even snacking on something. Nope, everyone just drinking and this place is starting to look like the place Marci told me to beware of. I decided after an hour I cannot wait until 7.30 p.m. which is the earliest meal service I could find, so bought a sandwich at the super Mercado and a packet of cookies and ate the lot in my pyjamas in bed... My knee is sore and boiling hot so I put cooling gel on and took another ArthoTec painkiller.

Day 28: Castaneda

Albergue Santiago Priv. 6 beds

Tuesday, September 17th, 2013   7.8km up and
down valleys

(Brierley says "we cross several shallow river valleys during these final stages so our path is more arduous than the contour plans might suggest. Ultreya!) right!
Dips and rises and poor signage out of Melide, made for an interesting day today. I walked awhile with Laura from Mexico, she is a Canadian but lives now in Mexico. We came upon a fantastic fruit stand in the woods, donativo again and we shared a packet of fresh sweet raspberries.
This Albergue is very hospitable, ran by a husband and wife team and their two children. I ordered lunch of scrambled eggs, salada, chips and water with my very limited Spanish. There is a washing machine here so I loaded all my gear into it but could find no detergent so I used hair shampoo. Next to the washer is a drier so today I can feel totally freshened with all clean and dry clothes. I am hoping there are no bed bugs though as I have a couple of bites on the back of my neck. I think that they are mosquitoes or flies, which are massive in Spain. It's like the pictures you see of Africa, with flies crawling all over everything. But I overheard a conversation of some pilgrims saying they found two bugs in their bed and they noted that some pilgrims never wash. Gawd, I never thought of that. Just in case, I have put my bed bug sheet under my sleeping bag.
Spanish salads seem to taste so much better, it's the combination of oil and vinegar and the vinegar is sweet, Todays salad was fresh curly lettuce, corn, tomatoes, tuna, finely grated carrots and white asparagus and topped off with three green olives. I am writing all this today because I have not a sole to talk to, I forgot to bring my crossword puzzle down here and the sole bunk mate (at present anyway) is an elderly surly Spaniard. He

did admittedly try to have a limited conversation with me when we first met, but quickly gave up in disgust at my poor Spanish and has now resorted to the daily newspaper.

Still, I am happy in this place and time, today was a peaceful walk among eucalyptus trees and the aroma so soothing, even to my knee.

Day 29: Arzua

Albergue da Fonte Priv. 20 beds

Wednesday, September 18th, 2013   6.1km   Ascent 100m

It's 1.30 p.m. and already I have my bed made up, have showered and done the laundry, walked around town twice and now have the rest of the day to relax. I am the only one checked in at this time and was the first again, so by good fortunes have snagged a bottom bunk.

I quite like Arzua, small town, very clean and orderly. It's hard to figure when the shops do business though; most shops are closed as I walked up and down the main street. Even after Siesta, most seem to be still closed. I saw some stunning leather clutch purses in a window, very reasonable prices. Marci and Josee would love them, but even if the shop was open, I cannot carry baggage at this stage.

It's concerning to see how the Spanish neglect their dogs, from the Albergue I hear pitiful nonstop barking, someone needs to let the poor thing out or in.

I found an internet station and booked my hotel at the Madrid airport. Also sent emails home.

An English elderly man has checked in now, he is very quiet, says he has stayed here before so is obviously doing the Camino again, or part thereof. Outside the rain has started, so my washing is not likely to dry today.

Only three days left and I shall be in Santiago! Tomorrow I am scheduled to walk 11km. and hope for the same good weather to continue.

Day 30: Salceda

Pousada de Salceda Priv. 10 beds

Thursday, September	11.1km + 7.8km when I
19th, 2013	missed the Pousada

Most of the walk today was on natural pathways and in the shade of the eucalyptus trees. It did start with a climb up to Arzua then down to three shallow river valleys before entering Salceda. My knee is complaining about them especially when I missed the road to Salceda and had to walk back 3.9km. Everyone shouting and laughing "You're going the wrong way."

Met Petra from Gores landing on one of the ups, she was moving at a snail pace like me. We walked together most of the day. We came upon another donativo stand, this time a Spanish man had two flats of fresh picked strawberries. We both indicated we would like a small dish and I offered four euros. At that, he emptied the whole flat into two bags and handed them to us. Totally aghast, we walked away offering strawberries to everyone on the path, the strawberries big and sweet and everyone loved them. We ended up parking ourselves on a stone wall to eat until we couldn't face another strawberry again then threw the last of them in the garbage, shame.

Salceda was way-off the trail and the pousada very poorly marked. According to Brierley it is directly on the trail, but it is a good 300m off, down a back country road which forks into two. Absolutely no indication what is down either lane. Fortunately I did not get far down the wrong path when I felt things were not right. The Albergue is brand new with extensive manicured grounds and showy waterfalls, a patio with chaise lounges and a bar patio featuring ultra-modern high glass tables and white leather stools. The restaurant has glass walls, a sleek bar and the same white leather and glass décor. There are high end hotel rooms across from the fountain and at the far end of the patio, a stone hacienda. This is the pilgrim house! Inside austere stone walls, no windows, metal bunks fitted close together. We are issued crisp white bedding at check-in. I made up my bunk, found a thick blanket in a large wooden cupboard and went to check out the shower (one for women and one for men.) The shower and adjoining washroom are the same stone walls and floor, but new-age fixtures where you need a degree in science to navigate the taps and glass shower door.

The reception is equally cold, even frosty. The woman at the reception desk was haughty and flippant and upset because she said the reservation was for "dos", I returned it was definitely for "una", but she went on and on about it and slapped the sheets on the pristine glass counter, then instantly disappeared outside still muttering "dos" and "una" to the presumed boss man/owner chappie and who it turned out was her husband. I called out if it was a problem I will pay for "dos" and she muttered something again jabbing her husband in the ribs. I told him disgustedly if it is a big problem I will pay for two, but I did not make the reservation. He assured me there was no problem and everything was fine and I was left still standing at the counter. Eventually he strolled back in and said he did not know I was there and finally directed me to the afore-mentioned hacienda at the back of the property (which I learned later was originally a cow shed). For all its glitz and glamour I was not at all impressed as I made my bed up but have decided to make a final comment tomorrow after I spend the night here. Walking 3.9km out of my way did not help the afternoon either.

Day 31: Pedrouzo

Albergue O Brugo Priv. 14 beds.

Friday, September 20th, 2013   7.9km   Ascent 105m

From Salceda, a climb to Alto de Santa Irene then steeply down to Arca and on to O Pedrouzo. Still quite a lovely walk, I just amble along, my knee is exquisitely painful today and had a poor sleep last night with constant pain in my knee. Add to that the huge variety of snoring and the woman in the bunk above me constantly getting up with a flashlight and rustling through her pack, I was glad when it was time to get up. The room was inky black, despite the ultra-modern attempt at sleekness. I really did not like the place at all and think here a private room would have been much better. The meals were very pricey and a fixed menu (two for peregrinos and one for "others.") but it is a captive audience, as we are out in the sticks so one has to eat here. I did anyway, have a totally lovely day with Denise from Ireland. We occupied a swing sofa opposite the fish ponds and fountains and chatted without taking a breath from 2.00 p.m. to 7.00 p.m. About 5.00 p.m we decided we were burning up so both dashed in to get towels to cover our legs and then continue where we left off. It was one of the best days of the Camino, a really super and relaxing afternoon. Denise is part of a tour group consisting of six Irish compatriots who started in Sarria. I just love these Irish!

I dragged myself over to the dining "palace" which I feel is really not designed with pilgrims in mind, but for the cruise ship model. The tourist group even changed for dinner. It was just about white glove service as we all sat in the same glass goldfish bowl. I ordered the pilgrim meal which is always too much for me, but there was no choice. The meal consisted of omelette with salad, chicken with fries (note fries again) ice cream and water (no wine thanks, I seldom take it) I sat alone and at the next table, another lady, also alone. I managed with my little French to start a small conversation and she in turn managed with her equally small English. But we did manage very well and agreed walking alone was very good, but evenings could be lonely. She said her son had walked with her until last week in Sarria when she also began solo as I had done. On my other side was a couple from Vancouver, Chris and Ann and we talked long into the evening. They are experienced hikers, having done the Pacific Coast, the Juan de Fuca, Kilimanjaro and the West Coast. I listened, a brilliant St. Patrick Green with envy. Chris told me to check out the Galloping Goose rail trail, 55km totally flat that connects with the Juan de Fuca. They have two children who they had just dropped off at University and were celebrating being now "footloose and fancy free."

At breakfast next morning I again sat next to the French lady and as we both started out on the trail, I introduced myself in my best French, "Je m'appelle Diane" and she laughed out loud "moi aussi", we both chuckled at such a funny coincidence.

I arrived here in O Pedrouzo one hour before the Albergue opened, so sat outside the door reading my Brierley. My knee is so painful I do not want to walk another inch. Two pilgrims have just gone by, one is wearing period garb of a long black cape and black hat and he looks like a character from medieval days. Right on noon the lady came to open up and welcomed me in with a big smile. She showed me the dorm and where the shower and laundry is. It didn't take long to get settled in and the kindly hospilatera has put all my laundry in the machine, so that within the hour I am lying in my bunk with nothing to do but rest my knee. While I was waiting outside for the Refugio to open I heard someone calling my name. At first I thought I was hearing things, but then I heard it again and looking up from my book, I saw Denise, across the road and frantically waving. Their group was also walking to Pedrouzo today. Denise says they will get to Santiago on the 22ⁿᵈ. Seems a lot of pilgrims will be 'landing' that day.

As usual, I don't hear too many people speaking English, it's mostly Spanish and German. However, as I spent most of the day lying on my bunk and reading, it doesn't really matter. The hospitalera came in with new pilgrims to settle in and as she went out, she came over and tickled my chin.

At 5.30 p.m. I went next door to the restaurant for something to eat, but of course, the earliest we can eat is 7.30 p.m. I am starving again and hate to wait so long. Three Irish ladies who are staying here are also in the restaurant, they like me hate having to wait so long. I joined them and we ate together, their lovely Irish lilt and sense of humour is welcome sounds to my ears.

Day 32: Monte Gozo

Saturday September 21ˢᵗ. 2013

Monte de Gozo	15.4km	Ascent 120m
municipal; 400 beds		

Today I am in agony with my knee, also very tired at the end, although I made good time and arrived at Monte Gozo at noon. There were about two dozen pilgrims waiting outside the reception block and the office doesn't open until 1.00 p.m. I sat on the grass in the shade of a tree, watching ants crawling all around me and hoping not to get too many bites, but it was either that or stand since the only two wooden benches were full. This place is like an army barracks, row upon row of blockhouses descending down a hill, beyond which lies the city of Santiago.

I left at 7.45 a.m. this morning and had my café con leche and danish in Pedrouzo. The path today crossed the busy N-547 several times, from then on it was pretty much a walk in the park, along woodland paths made fragrant by the heavy stands of euclalyptus. I climbed a bank to pluck a leaf and put it in my journal. The final assault up to Mont Gozo was a dreary slog on asphalt.

A middle aged couple went by early in the day that looked familiar, but I couldn't place them. The lady turned to me as she walked by and said "You've been walking a long time haven't you?"
"Does it show" I joked, as I was limping badly and going very slow.
"No", she said, "I remember you from a hundred miles ago." It was later I realised we first met at the wine fountain in Irache on Day eight and again in Viana on Day nine.
She and her husband waved hello again as I sat eating an apple on the church steps of Capela San Roque. I have not been able to

eat much, my stomach feels really upset and I feel a bit nauseous. Walking in this heat doesn't help much either, but Monte Gozo appeared surprisingly quickly. It is just beyond a picturesque little village, set up on a hill, with a huge monument to the Pope dominating the hill top and an open field behind that drops to the block houses. There is a bar in the village, well stocked with groceries, drinks and a little café with owners extremely helpful and pleasant who also speak English. Xacko Trans sent my bag to Lavacolla instead of here and the lady at the bar bent over backwards to call them and get it sent here tout suite. But I still had to sit around until 4.00 p.m. and wait for it to arrive; I could not shower or make my bunk up as everything is in that pack. Speaking of showers, they are the worst ever, not dirty, in fact very clean and new, but a half door, absolutely no hooks anywhere and only a tiny bench in the main toilet area to stack belongings. It's definitely walk out of the shower wrapped in a towel if you can. I had to go back to the village to pick up the pack, then back down to the village after my shower to take it back, as Xacko Trans does not pick up at the hostel. Consequently, I will not have a sleeping bag for tonight or a toiletry bag and headlamp, as they all go in the pack. I toyed with the idea of carrying my pack the 5km. tomorrow, but since I have no idea what the path is like and my knee is so painful, plus my stomach is still unsettled I decided best to have it sent to Santiago just in case.

After the shower, I put on all clean clothes to sleep in them and kept the ridiculously small and light backpacking towel as a blanket. No surprise I did not sleep a wink, I was freezing cold and the bunk was very uncomfortable. The room had eight beds and all were filled. I was eager to leave in the morning.
The reception, when we were finally let in was hilarious. Intimidating to start as two burly fully armed national guards watched us as we filed in. The receptionist, a man, spoke perfect German, Spanish and English and welcomed each one in turn in their own language. When it was my turn, he looked

at my passport and repeated my name out loudly, saying I was from "Ontahrrrio" rolling his r's in that guttural Spanish way. He said the fee would be 5€ but then winking and smilingly whispered in my ear "10€ for Quebec." He was the consummate joker, gave me my room number seven, "James Bond room" he said, "007."

As I went back to the village with my pack, I met Robin and Nellie who we had bunked with in Castrojerez. They had just arrived and were having supper in the café so I joined them but ordered toast only as I still feel very queasy. They had a big meal each of Salada and delicious looking Pizza, while I ate a single slice of toast. Robin said he and Bill his California friend had fallen out and were not speaking. I was surprised to hear that, they seemed to be such great friends when we met them and have been hiking together all their lives. Robin says he is not sure they can ever make amends.

Next surprise as I returned to my dorm I met Sherri from Seattle, we had a pilgrim meal with her on Day Two at Roncesvalles. The thing is, all these had walked the whole way and I felt very much like a cheat for having taken a bus at intervals.

Day 33: Santiago

Seminario San Marino

Sunday, September 22nd, 2013   5km.

I stopped at the large cafeteria on the Monto Gozo hill for a very pleasant breakfast of café con leche and fresh pastry before heading off to Santiago. I can see the lights of the city from this hill and it's a "pinch me" moment. The walk into the heart of the city was easy and I was joined part way by two men from England who were both walking for charity. As soon as I saw the Cathedral spire I felt awe struck, it was hard to sink in that here it is after so many days. And what seemed mere minutes I was in front of it, totally unable to process the whole scene. It was 9.15a.m. and I stood there thinking, I did it, it's done, it was relief, joy, excitement, sadness, happiness and every emotion piled on top. I found my way to the pilgrim office and joined the line-up for my Compestella. There I met Robin, Nellie, Bill, Sherri and at 9.45 a.m. I received my precious piece of paper. I fought back tears as it was handed to me with congratulations from the lady at the desk and again by the volunteer at the door who was leading people in. Dizzy with emotion and excitement, I stumbled into the side door of the Cathedral, just in time for the 10.00 a.m. pilgrim mass. A compelling holy service in Spanish and Latin, I felt dazed as I participated in the communion. Then, stunned to see them light the botofuemero, I couldn't believe my luck. All I had heard in the past few days was that this ceremony was not in practice anymore, except at the Friday evening mass. Some pilgrims even arranged to bus into Santiago for Friday night and be bussed back again to resume the walk. It is overwhelming in its splendour, something that will always be with me and the smell of the incense lingered in the Cathedral long after it was extinguished. The smell, the sight of it swinging so high, the organ that builds to a crescendo, was not unlike something from the Phantom of the Opera. Totally spectacular. I took pictures, but of course, nothing can equal being there.

Going back up to my room, who should be standing there waiting to check-in but Joanne and Jan. We stood staring and gaping at each other. Then screamed out "What are you doing here?" I last saw them on day three leaving Roncesvalles. They asked where Skai was and I told them she had left at Sarria. Jan gave me a big hug saying she was sorry the way things had turned out.

It is now 4.40 p.m. I am in my sparsely furnished little room at the nearby seminary, having had a shower and now rest comfortably in my single bed, which has crisp white sheets. My small but adequate bathroom has nice white towels. I no longer have to get up early in the morning and put my hiking boots on and I feel well satisfied that it is fait accompli. My stomach is still not well and I just ate a sandwich that has probably made me feel worse, but really, all is well with my world just now. From my small high window I can see Spanish rooftops and the wing of the seminary where the students are. There is a small cupola on the roof and the ancient bell there rings several times a day. Sometimes if I stand on tip toe I can almost see into one of the rooms at dawn, when the bell calls to matins. 'Ask not for whom the bell tolls, it tolls for thee' as Hemingway said. I am a little tired as I have walked around Santiago all afternoon, but I can relax now. I have just popped another pain killer and as I did so, suddenly realised, this is the cause of my queasy stomach. I have been knocking them back heavily these past few days, so now I am finished hiking, I am going to ease up on them. It's been altogether a memorable walk and an extraordinary experience.

DREAMSCAPE

When I think of soul nourishment and spiritual awareness I think of wilderness places. Places where tall pines stand like sentries, where crystal lakes reflect the sky and deep dark forests are home to the wild things, Deer, Moose, Bear, Beavers, Wolves.

Canoeing and portaging through Algonquin Park or Temagami, you leave the false world of cars planes and automobiles for the primal pursuit of just 'being'. We dip the oars in the water and touch our past, something in your bones tells you this is familiar, natural and we paddle instinctively. The steady trickle of water over paddles is the only sound as we glide along. At night on some remote shore a rude camp. It's a small nylon tent with just enough room for two sleeping bags. A simple meal is cooked over a prehistoric fire and our seats are the fallen logs of the forest. There are no taps, no flush toilets, we bring water from the lake and fill our water bottles in preparation for the journey tomorrow. Food is hung from overhead branches and we crawl into our sleeping bags to sleep like babies.

Morning brings another early start, loading our canoe we push out into the lake and head for the next portage. And so the rhythm continues, one day is like any other and for fourteen days we travel south and east. Long silent paddles and rocky portages give room for introspection; life is reduced to its simplest form. Where shall I sleep tonight? And what will I eat?

Otters play in the lake, Moose eat reeds in the shallows and Bear tracks on the trail alert us to be watchful.

At night, sitting on a rocky outcrop, we gaze at the galaxy of stars, at the further shores of the lake marked by a black line of the tall pines and there is a peaceful hush. A bright yellow moon peeps over the trees and reflects in the still waters below. Alone in this remote wilderness our voices echo round the shores and come back to us, There is moonlight and mystery and wonder.

It is a spiritual journey as well as a physical one. I feel at peace out here walking among the tall sombre pines, standing by a thundering waterfall, or plying the crystal lakes. Algonquin Park has been called "A twentieth century cathedral for the soul" it has been my solace. To finally come 'out' into the glare of highways and humanity is an assault to the senses and will take a few days to get used to.

I think that I should retreat back into the forest for ever.

RITUALS

My wedding took place at the end of August. I looked forward to the day with happy anticipation but also with a profound sense of self awareness. It was a second wedding and seemed so much more than its sum, at once intense and simple. Everything was brought down to a basic rite of passage, I am more aware this time, more in touch with who and where I am in life's drama. No church wedding; our cathedral is the wilderness and forests, our alter the steps of the old "Corran" *Gaelic meaning, "the point of land running into the sea."* Because we both love nature and because I had hiked the whole of the Bruce Trail, it was decided that this was where we wanted to be married. Hidden in the shade of trees up on the Georgian Bay the old ruin sits in a heavenly glade, where squirrel's perch on branches, birds flit from tree to tree and the air is scented with pine.

A young minister who shared our love of nature was only too delighted to conduct a ceremony amongst this natural backdrop. The aisle, a narrow woodland path, was walked along with my daughter; daughter-in-law, three grandchildren and a special niece. Rachel at ten months old was carried by her mom, Liam aged seven acted as ring bearer and Emma, aged three and Clara at five were the flower girls, both carrying tiny straw baskets of the wild flowers. Niece Kate proudly was my maid of honour. To the strains of "Mull of Kintyre" family sat or stood about, as did fellow hikers of the Bruce Trail. A brief sermon was read comparing long hiking paths with their trials and trophies to the long path of marriage.
Standing together in dappled sunlight, under a blue vermillion sky, we exchanged simple vows and golden wedding bands. After the short and simple ceremony, bottles of bubbly wine popped, cheers rang out and my hiker friends declared this "the wedding of the century."

The sun shone down on us, the breeze murmured in the trees, birds sang, children played amongst the ruins and I enjoyed a short stroll with my son to the edge of the cliff where we looked down on the vast blue waters of Georgian Bay.

Hours later found us heading to the nearby peninsula, to enjoy good food, good friends and family.

One of my favourite trees is the Tamarack, its vivid gold in autumn illuminating many a northern landscape. How fitting it is then, that here I stand at the end of a golden day on small point of land called Tamarack Island!

Speech

I copy here, by kind permission of Nicholas, the speech he gave at our dinner at the Tamarac Inn.

"We are gathered here today to celebrate a unique relationship between my mom and Richie.

Richie, I've only known you for a few years, whereas I've had a lifetime relationship with my mom. So here's a list of pointers that I think you'll find helpful in the long days and weeks ahead.....

1. When my mom comes home from a long day at the office, cheer her up by telling her you really want to spend the evening watching figure skating championship on TV over and over and over again.

2. Try to become the oldest living member of the Youth Hostel Association

3. Schedule a weekend hiking trip to Mt. Kilimanjaro

4. Read and memorize the complete works of Grey Owl

5. Always keep a Mars bar handy in case the going gets tough

6. No hunt camp could ever be complete without

   a. Grecian statues

   b. S shaped hedges

   c. 3 swimming pools

7. Since my mom has been thoroughly trained in the operation and maintenance of a chain saw she commands respect. Feel free to invite her to participate in land clearing expeditions, or other camp hunt renovations where the use of a 48" bar chain saw is necessary.

8. Learn and be able to perform on command at least three basic ballet positions.

9. If you need an energy boost, try a sugar sandwich, they're nutritious really.

10. Your previous experience as a firefighter should make you ideally suited to life with mom. She may be a small package, but the contents can be highly explosive.

Mom, based on my knowledge of Richie, I've got a few pointers for you too.

1. Golf is a game where small hard balls are struck with a club; try to limit this activity to the fairway.

2. I encourage you to get out and play some golf with him. If you hit a few bad shots just remember to shout out your height in feet to alert other players in the area of a hazardous ball.

3. Since Richie is an avid hunter, it's important you understand the true origins of hunters. These people were traditionally organized into small nomadic groups where women collected food while men hunted. At one time all humans probably lived this way but now only a few groups remain, such as the Australian aboriginals. So next time you are out picking blueberries and Richie's dragging home dinner, remember that you are truly two of a kind.

SIGHT

All around me the summer is fading far too quickly. The flower boxes of bright pink busy Lizzies and blue lobelias have turned to a tangle of brown, like faded tiny birds sitting on limp dull stems. The trailing ivies are shedding their glossy green leaves and lay as if exhausted. On telephone wires and tree tops, great gangs of birds congregate in busy assemblage, fluffing feathers and ready to fly south and leave us to the cold winter. Maples nod gently in the soft breeze, decked out in new autumn colours of flaming reds and shimmering yellows. Tamarac's will wait to compete, turning rich green needles to shining gold before laying them at her feet for a carpet. The sun is in a race with the clouds that are bent on turning the skies to a gloomy shade of grey.

SOUND

There is a lull in the air, a breath between seasons. We don't hear the twittering and cooing of birds quite as much, leaves faintly rustle to the ground and squirrels scamper, busy building a summer cache. The loon no longer sings on the lake. Summer has gone to sleep and autumn has reached low ebb. In the distance, the whine of a chain saw, Dwayne is sawing logs for his winter fire. The hum of bicycle tires speeds on the road, lean bodies, shoulders bent into the wind, peddles grinding, straining up hills and free-wheeling down the other side, the wheels hum. I sit at the table, pen scratching across the page, trying to put my thoughts on paper as I listen to the "Ave Verum" sung by an Oxford choir. It is a slow piece, reverend, peaceful, soothing yet delving deep into the soul. A choir of voices, a chant, it is by Mozart and sometimes I cannot bear to listen, it is almost cruel in its beauty. Its loneliness, purity of voice, intones solitude and sanctity, the slip to a minor key, is transcending and I know as long as I can hear music, nothing can ever overcome me. It sings strength and a calmness of spirit. I am, therefore I am.

ITHAKA

As you set out for Ithaka
hope that your journey is a long one,
full of adventure, full of discovery.
Laestrygonians and Cyclops,
angry Poseidon-don't be afraid of them:
you'll never find things like that on your way
as long as you keep your thoughts raised high,
as long as a rare sensation
touches your spirit and your body.
Laestrygonians and Cyclops,
wild Poseidon-you won't encounter them
unless you bring them along inside your soul,
unless your soul sets them up in front of you.

Hope that your journey is a long one.
May there be many summer mornings when,
with what pleasure, what joy,
you come into harbors you're seeing for the first time;
may you stop at Phoenician trading stations
to buy fine things,
mother of pearl and coral, amber and ebony,
sensual perfume of every kind-
as many sensual perfumes as you can;
and may you visit many Egyptian cities
to learn and learn again from those who know.

Keep Ithaka always in your mind.
Arriving there is what you're destined for.
But don't hurry the journey at all.
Better if it lasts for years,
so that you're old by the time you reach the island,
wealthy with all you've gained on the way,
not expecting Ithaka to make you rich.
Ithaka gave you the marvelous journey.
Without her you would have not set out.
She has nothing left to give you now.

And if you find her poor, Ithaka won't have fooled you.
Wise as you will have become, so full of experience,
you'll have understood by then what these Ithakas mean.

AFTERWORD

My grandmother, Eliza Ann Clarke (Clarke with an "e" as she always stated), was a childhood idol. During her lifetime I spent countless hours in her company and at age seventeen went to live with her. She exuded unconditional love and affability and was the best of companions with an acerbic wit. "Giv 'em some music, they want to dance!" she jeered, while watching boxing matches on television. I laughed quickly and easily at her caustic easy asides. In pretend bossy tones she would shout loudly to Uncle Bob (her husband)

"Put some coal on the fire Bob!"

"You want me to put some coal on the fire Liza?" he asked meekly.

Because he had lost his hearing in the Second World War, he often repeated his instructions, to make sure he had got them right.

Then in a flash, the prickly retort:

"O' course I do, you don't keep a dog and bark ya'self d'ya?"

She was short, round as a dumpling and easy-going. Nestled in her arms was like being wrapped in a warm down comforter. But I felt a distant sadness lingered about her at times. It was her eyes, the windows of the soul, deep and melancholy; my grandmother's eyes told of something forlorn or perhaps lost. Even while she cooed and laughed, you just couldn't help noticing the sad eyes. I remember her telling me one day that the barman at the local pub had once said to her "Don't let it make you bitter!" My child brain wondered. What did he mean? What would make her bitter? There was never any explanation. I know her second husband, a fisherman, was killed at sea during the Second World War. Every November, on Remembrance Day, we turned on the television as the Queen laid a wreath on the cenotaph in London. With glassy eyes she pretended to be busy fixing a clock or knitting. "What do they want to show that for?" she barked, "Nobody cares." But then turning to me, she repeated the fateful conversation, "They knocked on the door, they said: 'Mrs. Clarke, there was smoke on the first day there was smoke on the second day but there was no smoke on the third day'. This is in reference to my Uncle Leo, her second husband. He was out on the North Sea when the trawler he was on was sunk; a casualty of war. My Uncle Leo's name is on that London cenotaph, you can find it, "L. Corcoran" under the trawler name *"Bromelia"* which sailed out of Grimsby. I had just been born at that time and mom tells me Uncle Leo came to visit me before he sailed, "When I come back that baby will have the biggest teddy bear in Grimsby" he swelled. But he never came back. I think this is the sadness in my grandmother's eyes.

But there is more; if Uncle Leo was the second husband, who was the first? It's a secret. I've heard whispers, something about gran being pregnant before being married. It was a topic secretive and unmentionable. The result of that pregnancy was my father. I found out she was made to marry a man called Thompson. Who was he and who was my father's real father? In his failing years my father asks me to copy a poem out for him, he frames it and hangs it on the living room wall. It is called *"For my Da."* It's about a son who aches for a father who left home and my father weeps at the lines. I am left to wonder and question and in my father's dementia he begins to ramble of the day he saw his father walk away. It's a stark picture and clearly my father has, over the years, carried a deep and private grief. I listen to the story and after all these years some of that mystery is gradually revealed. I find that my father's paternal father was a naval officer who came from Glasgow and as an infant my father became a pawn in the age old battle of custody and taken to that city to live. But being the child of separate parents, a struggle ensued and after several years was again taken back to England. A young officer, came to visit his child of five, only to find a different order and that in his absence, a seaman by the name of Leo had taken up residence. "You are wearing my tie" cried Roy Campbell. This became the match that set the fire and a terrible fight ensued that fell out into the street. The result was that Roy Campbell walked away and into the pages of history. But my father, broken hearted, will cling to this last image of his father leaving and in his memory my brother is christened Roy Campbell, in addition, my sister and I will be given a middle name of Campbell.

I heard my grandmother was sent away in disgrace for a while to London, "to visit an aunt" I think was the official explanation. The man called Thompson I find was elderly and that arranged marriage was quickly annulled. I see now the sadness in my grandmother's eyes. The whole affair has been an off-limits subject and it seemed my grandmother was an outcast. I wish I could have talked to my grandmother about it all. I feel a great sadness for her when I learn these stories. I wish she had kept a journal so that I can have a glimpse into her life, what she did, what she liked, where did she go, where was she in London? How did she meet Roy Campbell? Why did she cling to an abusive relationship with Leo?

I want to know these answers but I will not have them. For these reasons and many more, I feel it is important that we should try to leave a story of some sort for future generations to read, to tell who their ancestors were. Who were they? What happened to them and what was their life like? My father has traced our ancestors back to the workhouses of the 1800's. What was their daily routine, did they live there all their lives, what kind of clothes did they wear, what did they eat, why were they in the workhouse?

I persuaded both of my parents to write an autobiography. I believe it is important for future generations that we carry these histories forward. My parents lived and survived the ravages of a country at war, living was hard, food was short, life was uncertain. Today's generation know little of that time and its challenges. Now at least, there is one generation in our family that has some kind of record, should they ever feel the urge to enquire about where and from whom they have their origin.

Similarly, I have endeavoured to keep a journal on a regular basis, partly because I like to write, but also, because I want to leave something informative for my offspring. Something, that in some quiet moment of reflection, they may wish to know something of who I really am. Where and how did I live, where did I work and especially about my travels. Maybe it will ignite a spark and they will travel too. I shall be long gone then, but at least if they ever should question, "Who is that?" Someone can then turn them to this modest little book and they will see the answer: It is me! I who was once a young child like you, who became a mother and then a grandmother. I, of whom it can be said, am a living contradiction; impulsive, inconsistent, extravagant, stubborn and subject to quick changes of mood, but also modest, adventurous, generous, refined, loyal, sentimental, sensitive and tenacious. I know what failure is, I know how it feels to be disliked. I have suffered abandonment, abuse, but I have also gained strength which each battle fought and won, I am a survivor and I learned how to reclaim my life from a lonely place. My life has had many twists and turns, some parts have been exquisitely painful, others euphoric in their magnificence. How about you? Who are you? What do you like? Where will your life journey take you?

Life can change in a wink, don't waste a precious moment, savour the morning sun as it climbs over the horizon, count the stars and write your own story. There is nothing you can't do, no obstacle that cannot be surmounted. You are the sum of workhouses of the 1800's, of survivors; seamen, fishermen, engineers, musicians, housemaids, adventurers, your roots lie in Scotland, England and Norway. Add now with confidence, your own distinctive story to the, the tree of life. *Carpe-diem*

BIBLIOGRAPHY

(Butterfly Bombs terror | Grimsby Telegraph n.d.). n.d.

(http://en.wikipedia.org/wiki/Sten n.d.). n.d.

(Rationing in the United Kingdom n.d.). n.d.

Air-Raid Shelter. n.d. http://en.wikipedia.org/wiki/ Morrison_shelter (accessed April 2014).

Anderson Shelter-Spartacus Educational. n.d. http://spartacus-educational.com/2WWandersonshelter.htm.

Brierley, John. "A Pilgrims Guide to the Ca.m.ino de Santiago." Findhorn Press Ltd., n.d.

Butterfly Bombs terror | Grimsby Telegraph. n.d. http://www. grimsbytelegraph.co.uk/Butterfly-Bombs-terror/story-19270886-detail/story.html.

Emerson, Ralph Waldo. n.d. http://thinkexist.com/quotation/ to_laugh_often_and_much-to_win_the_respect_of/255196. html.

http://en.wikipedia.org/wiki/Sten. n.d.

Proverbial Phrases. n.d. http://en.wikipedia.org/wiki/ List_of_proverbial_phrases#P.

Rationing in the United Kingdom. n.d. http://en.w wikipedia.org/ wiki/Rationing_in_the_United_Kingdom.

virtue, Patience is a. *Proverbial Phrases.* n.d. http://en.wikipedia.
org/wiki/List_of_proverbial_phrases#P.

Ithaka Poem;C.P. Cavafy. *C.P. Cavafy: Selected Poems.*
Translated by Edmund Keeley and Philip Sherrard. ©
1992 Edmund Keeley and Philip Sherrard. Reprinted by
permission of Princeton University Press.

(h t t p : / / e n . w i k i p e d i a . o r g / w i k i /
History_of_the_Knights_Templar n.d.)